The Cambridge Liturgical Psalter

The Cambridge Liturgical Psalter

John Emerton
David Frost
Andrew Macintosh

The Lutterworth Press

The Lutterworth Press
P.O. Box 60
Cambridge
CB1 2NT
United Kingdom

www.lutterworth.com
publishing@lutterworth.com

Paperback ISBN: 978 0 7188 9771 0
PDF ISBN: 978 0 7188 9772 7
ePub ISBN: 978 0 7188 9773 4

British Library Cataloguing in Publication Data
A record is available from the British Library

First published by William Collins and the Church Information Office, 1976
This edition published by The Lutterworth Press, 2024

Copyright © David L Frost, John A Emerton, Andrew A Macintosh 1976, 1977, 2012, 2013, 2024

All rights reserved. No part of this edition may be reproduced, stored electronically or in any retrieval system, or transmitted in any form or by any means, electronic, mechanical, photocopying, recording, or otherwise, without prior written permission from the Publisher (permissions@lutterworth.com).

Contents

The Translators	vii
Introduction to the New Edition	ix
Introduction	xiv
The Psalms	1

The Translators

Hebrew Panel

Sebastian P. Brock, M.A., D.Phil., University Lecturer in Aramaic and Syriac, and Fellow of Wolfson College, Oxford (Church of England).

The Rev. J. A. Emerton, M.A., D.D. (Chairman), Regius Professor of Hebrew, and Fellow of St John's College, Cambridge (Church of England).

The Rev. William Horbury, M.A., Ph.D., Vicar of Great Gransden; formerly Fellow of Clare College, Cambridge; Examining Chaplain to the Bishop of Peterborough (Church of England).

The Rev. John F. McHugh, L.S.S., Ph.L., S.T.D., Lecturer in Theology, University of Durham; formerly Director of Studies and Lecturer in Sacred Scripture at Ushaw College, Durham (Roman Catholic).

The Rev. A. A. Macintosh, M.A. (Secretary), Fellow, Tutor and Assistant Dean of St John's College, Cambridge; Examining Chaplain to the Bishop of Carlisle (Church of England).

The Rev. A. G. MacLeod, M.A., Principal of Westminster College, Cambridge; formerly Moderator of the Presbyterian Church of England (United Reformed Church).

The Rev. Ernest W. Nicholson, M.A., B.D., Ph.D., University Lecturer in Divinity, and Fellow and Dean of Pembroke College, Cambridge (Church of England).

John G. Snaith, M.A., B.D., University Lecturer in Hebrew and Aramaic, Cambridge, Member of the Faith and Order Committee of the Methodist Church; Local Preacher (Methodist).

English

David L. Frost, M.A., Ph.D., Professor of English, University of Newcastle, New South Wales; formerly Fellow of St John's College, Cambridge; member of the Church of England Liturgical Commission (Church of England).

Introduction to the New Edition

The integrity of this translation of the Psalms in modern English consists in the mode of its creation: it was made completely anew. Accordingly, it is not a revision of an older version, as were most other modern language psalters of the twentieth century. This version was commissioned in 1972 by the Liturgical Commission of the Church of England with the approval of the Archbishops of Canterbury and York and was incorporated in the official *Alternative Services Book* of 1980.

The work in completing this translation lasted eight years. It was undertaken by a panel, convened for the purpose, under the chairmanship of J.A. Emerton, the then Regius Professor of Hebrew in the University of Cambridge[1]. The panel consisted of eight Hebrew specialists and one scholar of English Literature, D.L. Frost. The Hebraists were largely Anglicans but included members of the Roman Catholic, Methodist and United Reform Churches. It is noteworthy that the differences of Christian allegiance did not in any way affect the way in which the problems of translation were tackled.

This translation was intended to be used within churches, as a version which would express the meaning of the psalms clearly in modern English. This translation also benefitted from the fact that study of the language and of the textual problems of the Hebrew Bible had advanced considerably in the preceding decades. More was known about the meanings of Hebrew words and the history of the text of the Hebrew Bible, and techniques had been developed for dealing with obscure passages and verses where it is probable that

---

1. See p. xyz for a full list of members of the panel, described in regard to the positions they held in the 1970s, the time of the working sessions.

mistakes were made by scribes copying the text by hand in ancient times.

The method deployed by the translation panel

The first step in preparing the translation was for one of the Hebrew scholars to draft a rendering of a psalm, and for his draft to be discussed and revised by the others. The second draft thus reflected the judgment not just of one scholar but of a team of scholars with a specialized knowledge of Hebrew and of the Old Testament. Such team work was indicative of the breadth of knowledge that was available and precluded the inclusion of fads favoured by individual members. At this stage, the goal was simply to indicate the meaning of the original, rather than to achieve a style acceptable in English or aim for literary elegance. While for the most part the meaning of the Psalms is clear, there are some obscure passages, such as Psalm 87, where the panel was obliged to hazard a translation which seemed to make sense in the context. There are also places where the inability to achieve good sense is a likely result of scribal mistakes in ancient times, and here the translators felt free to make small corrections to the Hebrew text. They were, however, reluctant to make changes except where there was no satisfactory alternative. They were also cautious about accepting new meanings for Hebrew words which were unsupported by reasonable evidence.

The second stage was the responsibility of David Frost. He took the agreed draft and prepared a rendering in an English style and rhythm suitable for use in church. His translation came back to the panel, who were free to criticize it if they thought that it misrepresented the meaning of the Hebrew or if they were dissatisfied with the English wording. They did not themselves alter Frost's version, but asked him to consider their representations and to bring back a revision to the panel. It was thus the aim, on the one hand, to gain the considered opinion of the Hebraists and, on the other, to avoid the flatness of what has been described as 'committee English'.

This process ensured that this translation remains a fresh rendering of the Hebrew into modern English, not a revision of an older version. However, the panel was not inclined to novelty for its own sake, and they were free to make use of many phrases from earlier translations. Moreover, they followed the example of the great translators of the sixteenth and seventeenth centuries who reproduced many of the images and idioms of the original Hebrew. Lively expressions modelled on the Hebrew were deemed preferable to tired expressions and clichés drawn from vernacular English. Slight archaisms were deployed in recognition of the fact that the original text came from ancient Israel, but they were tested concerning their intelligibility for those who might have been unfamiliar with them or with older English versions. Every effort was made to render the Psalms into language that ordinary Christians could understand.

The Status of the translated Psalms

The Alternative Service book, in which the Psalms were incorporated, had a run of almost twenty years. In the 1990s, however, the Church of England Commission engaged in further liturgical revision. Where the Psalms were concerned, the Commission proposed to adopt another version, at the time in use by the English Franciscan order. The version was subsequently named *The Psalter 1998*. This decision was curious and somewhat surprising. The translation was originally produced by a committee of the Episcopal Church of the U.S.A in the 1960s, and went through several revisions for successive American prayer books. It is not known whether qualified Hebraists were involved, but the primary purpose seems to have been to revise the familiar Psalms of the *Book of Common Prayer*[2] to accord with the need for modern English and for inclusive language. The poet W.H. Auden, who had been involved in the project, reported in a private communication that he had done his best to preserve as much of the old wording as possible. The version 'ended up neither Tudor nor modern English but a clumsy hybrid'[3].

The Commission had resolved, as early as 1971, to give no further consideration to this version in their continuing work of liturgical revision. Yet, by 1997, the version resurfaced as the preferred option for the future official psalter of the Church of England.

---

2. This much-loved version, produced by Miles Coverdale in the 1530s, was a translation of a Latin text of the Psalms and not at all a rendering of the Hebrew original.
3. See *A Daft Text*, p.2.

At this stage, three members of the translation panel of the *Liturgical Psalter*, J.A., Emerton, D.L. Frost and A.A. Macintosh[4], published a detailed criticism of the revived American version. The work included verses from both the psalters in contention, set out side by side. The booklet was entitled[5], *A Daft Text: the Psalter 1998*[6].

These and other severe criticisms of the proposed psalter resulted in the Commission inviting two competent Hebraists (A. Gelston and J. Rogerson) to renovate the version, removing all the many glaring mistakes and infelicities. This was akin, as it has been said, to taking over a ramshackle house, renovating it without benefit of professional architects and then calling in professionals to put things right after the event. This is in stark contrast to the translation of *The Liturgical Psalter*, crafted completely *de novo*.

Much of the impetus for the adoption of *The Psalter 1998* arose from the claim that it was closer to Coverdale's version of the *Book of Common Prayer*. Yet examination of the version alongside *The Liturgical Psalter* suggested that *The Psalter 1998* uses 9% more of Coverdale's words than *The Liturgical Psalter*, though it preserves substantially more of his mistranslations[7].

Despite these concerns, *The Psalter 1998* was formally adopted by the Church of England as the official psalter and incorporated in the definitive *Common Worship* (2000).

The Liturgical Psalter, however, remains a version fully authorized for use in the Church of England. It was incorporated in *An Australian Prayer Book* (1978), in an *Alternative Prayer Book* (1984) in the Church of Ireland, and in *An Anglican Prayer Book* in the Church of the Province of South Africa. It has been reprinted in a variety of publications in England and overseas, adopted for use by the Uniting Church of Australia and excerpted for the Methodist *Hymns and Psalms* (1983). In 1996, *The Liturgical Psalter* was extensively excerpted

---

4. Two other scholars, members of the panel, who did not take part in composing the booklet, wished their names to be associated with its contents: W. Horbury and E.W. Nicholson.
5. The title *A Daft Text* derives from a review of the new translation in *News of the Liturgy* (April, 1999). The printer's devil seems to have become here, providentially, a printer's angel.
6. *A Daft Text: the Psalter 1998*, Aquila Books: Cambridge and Sydney, 1999.
7. See further, *A Daft Text*, p.4.

Introduction to the New Edition   xiii

in Donald Davie's edition of the Penguin Classics *The Psalms in English*, as one of two versions representative of the twentieth century.

Publishing History

1977. *The Psalms: A New Translation for Worship.* William Collins and the Church Information Office.
1995. *The Liturgical Psalter (New Inclusive Language Version).* HarperCollins.
1995. *A Prayer Book for Australia.* Broughton Publishing.
2012. *The Cambridge Liturgical Psalter*[8]. Aquila Books.

1995. Note: A Roman Catholic document *The Liturgical Psalter* (International Consultation on English in the Liturgy) was published using the same name as the original *Liturgical Psalter* of 1977 (as above). The imprimatur for the work was revoked in 1998 by the (R.C.) Church because of 'concerns about the doctrinal accuracy of the translation'. Since the original *Liturgical Psalter* of 1977 is permitted for use in the Church of England, the copyright holders took the opportunity to avoid any possible confusion by renaming the latter *The Cambridge Liturgical Psalter*.

A.A. Macintosh
Secretary of the Translation Panel

---

8. This edition of *The Liturgical Psalter* includes notes written by the Secretary of the translation panel. They were designed to give some account of differences between the new translation and that of Coverdale in the *Book of Common Prayer*. Some comparison has been made with other translations of the Psalms, including, e.g., the *New English Bible*. The notes were written at the request of the Chairman of the Liturgical Commission to meet the needs of persons who were not Hebraists. While they should not be regarded as a full and comprehensive commentary on the textual and philological decisions of the panel, a number of correspondents have found them helpful.

Introduction

The Psalms

Christians have used the Psalms in their praises of God, in their prayers and in their meditations since the earliest days of the Church. The Jews have used the Psalms for a much longer time, for they were composed for use in ancient Israel. The majority of the Psalms are hymns of praise and thanksgiving to God for what he is and for what he has done (e.g Ps. 8, 104, 135), or prayers for help and laments because of the sufferings of an individual (e.g. Ps. 6, 22) or his anxieties (e.g Ps. 77), or because of some national disaster such as defeat in battle (e.g. Ps. 44) or the destruction of Jerusalem and its temple (e.g. Ps. 74, 79). There are also meditations on God's providence (e.g. Ps. 49, 73, 78) or on his commandments (e.g. Ps. 1, 119). Other Psalms were composed for particular occasions in the nation's life: for the accession of a new king (Ps. 2), for a royal wedding (Ps. 45), or for a pilgrimage to Jerusalem to worship at the temple (e.g. Ps. 84, 122). The temple was the place where most Psalms were originally intended to be sung, but they also came to be used by Jewish congregations in their synagogues and by individuals in their private prayers.

The period in which the Psalms were composed in ancient Israel goes back as early as the time of King David (c. 1000 BC), though modern scholars have questioned the tradition that he was the author of a large number of the poems in our Psalter. Some Psalms were certainly written much later: Ps. 137, for instance, speaks of the exile of the Jews from Jerusalem to Babylon in the sixth century BC. Most of the Psalms, however cannot be dated precisely and might have been written at almost any time within a period of several centuries. Nor do we know when the last poem in the Psalter was written, though

Introduction

it was probably not later than about 200 BC and may well have been much earlier. The Psalms thus reflect something like three quarters of a millennium in the life and worship of ancient Israel.

Jesus was born a Jew, and he was brought up to know the Psalms intimately and to ponder them. He quoted them in his teaching, and words from the Psalter were on his lips as he hung on the cross. The Church learned from him, and from God's ancient people the Jews, to value the Psalms, and Christians have used them ever since.

When Christians read the Psalms, they meditate and share the thoughts and varied emotions of the people of God in the Old Testament, the people to whom God made himself known, and they share in Israel's experience of God. The God of the Psalms is the God and Father of our Lord Jesus Christ. The coming of Christ has, however, made a difference, and Christians cannot always think of God in exactly the same way as those who lived before the birth, and death, and resurrection of Jesus. Christians cannot make their own everything in the Psalter, at least not in its original sense. We cannot, for example, identify ourselves with the author of Ps. 137 when he blesses those who will dash Babylonian children against the rocks, however well we may understand the Psalmist's reaction to the murder by Babylonian soldiers of Jewish children. There are parts of the Psalter that Christians must read with detachment. Many Christians feel that they must go further and refrain from the use of such passages, at least in public worship. Nevertheless, although there are verses in the Psalter whose sentiments Christians must not share, there remains much more which they can wholeheartedly make their own.

Throughout the centuries, Christians of different persuasions have found the Psalms a means of prayer and worship that fulfilled their needs. In the future, as in the past, Christians will use the Psalms both in the public worship of the Church and in their private devotions, in meditation, in prayer, and, above all, in praise.

Psalm 1

1. Blessed is the man
     who has not walked in the counsel of the ungodly:
   nor followed the way of sinners,
     nor taken his seat amongst the scornful.

2. But his delight is in the law of the Lord:
     and on that law will he ponder day and night.

3. He is like a tree planted beside streams of water:
     that yields its fruit in due season.

4. Its leaves also shall not wither:
     and look, whatever he does, it shall prosper.

5. As for the ungodly, it is not so with them:
     they are like the chaff which the wind scatters.

6. Therefore the ungodly shall not stand up at the judgement:
     nor sinners in the congregation of the righteous.

7. For the Lord cares for the way of the righteous:
     but the way of the ungodly shall perish.

Psalm 2

1. Why are the nations in tumult:
     and why do the peoples cherish a vain dream?

2. The kings of the earth rise up and the rulers conspire together:
     against the Lord and against his anointed, saying,

3. 'Let us break their bonds asunder:
     let us throw off their chains from us.

4. He that dwells in heaven shall laugh them to scorn:
     the Lord will hold them in derision.

5. Then will he speak to them in his wrath,
     and terrify them in his fury:
   'I, the Lord, have set up my king on Zion my holy hill.'

6. I will announce the Lord's decree,
     that which he has spoken:
   'You are my son, this day have I begotten you.

7. 'Ask of me,
    and I will give you the nations for your inheritance:
  the uttermost parts of the earth for your possession.

8. 'You shall break them with a rod of iron:
    and shatter them in pieces like a potter's vessel.'

9. Now therefore be wise, O kings:
    be advised, you that are judges of the earth.

10. Serve the Lord with awe,
    and govern yourselves in fear and trembling:
  lest he be angry, and you perish in your course.

11. For his wrath is quickly kindled:
    blessed are those that turn to him for refuge.

Psalm 3

1. Lord, how numerous are my enemies:
    many they are that rise against me.

2. Many there are that talk of me and say:
    'There is no help for him in his God.'

3. But you, Lord, are about me as a shield:
    you are my glory, and the lifter up of my head.

4. I cry to the Lord with a loud voice:
    and he answers me from his holy hill.

5. I lay myself down and sleep:
    I wake again, because the Lord sustains me.

6. Therefore I will not be afraid
      of the multitudes of the nations:
  who have set themselves against me on every side.

7. Arise, Lord, and deliver me, O my God:
    for you will strike all my enemies upon the cheek,
  you will break the teeth of the ungodly.

8. Deliverance belongs to the Lord:
    O let your blessing be upon your people.

Psalm 4

1. Answer me when I call, O God of my righteousness:
    when I was hard-pressed you set me free;
  be gracious to me now and hear my prayer.

2. Sons of men, how long will you turn my glory to my shame:
    how long will you love what is worthless and seek after lies?

3. Know that the Lord has shown me his wonderful kindness:
    when I call to the Lord he will hear me.

4. Tremble, and do no sin:
    commune with your own heart upon your bed and be still.

5. Offer the sacrifices that are right:
    and put your trust in the Lord.

6. There are many who say 'Who will show us any good?:
    the light of your countenance, O Lord, has gone from us.'

7. Yet you have given my heart more gladness:
    than they have when their corn, wine and oil increase.

8. In peace I will lie down and sleep:
    for you alone, Lord, make me dwell in safety.

Psalm 5

1. Hear my words, O Lord, give heed to my groaning:
    listen to my cry, you that are my king and my God.

2. In the morning when I pray to you,
    surely you will hear my voice:
  at daybreak I lay my prayers before you, and look up.

3. For you are not a God who takes pleasure in wickedness:
    nor can any evil dwell with you.

4. The boastful cannot stand in your sight:
    you hate all those that work mischief.

5. Those who speak lies you destroy:
    you abhor the treacherous, O Lord,
  and those that are stained with blood.

6. But because of your great goodness
    I will come into your house:
  I will bow down toward your holy temple
    in awe and fear of you.

7. Lead me, O Lord, in your righteousness,
    for my enemies lie in wait:
  make straight your way before me.

8. For there is no truth in their mouth:
    and within they are eaten up by malice.

9. Their throat is an open sepulchre:
    and their tongue speaks smooth and flattering words.

10. Destroy them, O God,
     let them fall by their own contriving:
   cast them out for their many offences,
     for they have rebelled against you.

11. But let all who put their trust in you rejoice:
     let them shout with joy for ever.

12. Be the defender of those who love your name:
     let them exult because of you.

13. For you will bless, O Lord, the man that is righteous:
     you will cover him with your favour as with a shield.

Psalm 6

1. O Lord, rebuke me not in your indignation:
    nor chasten me in your fierce displeasure.

2. Have mercy upon me, O Lord, for I am weak:
    O Lord, heal me, for my very bones are afraid.

3. My soul also is greatly troubled:
    and you, Lord—how long will you delay?

4. Turn again, O Lord, and deliver my soul:
    O save me for your mercy's sake.

5. For in death no man remembers you:
    and who can give you thanks from the grave?

6. I am wearied with my groaning:
    every night I drown my bed with weeping,
  and water my couch with my tears.

7. My eyes waste away for sorrow:
    they grow dim because of all my enemies.

8. Away from me, all you that do evil:
    for the Lord has heard the voice of my weeping.

9. The Lord has heard my supplication:
    the Lord will receive my prayer.

10. All my enemies shall be put to shame and greatly dismayed:
    they shall turn back and be confounded in a moment.

Psalm 7

1. O Lord my God, to you have I come for shelter:
    save me from all who pursue me, O save and deliver me,

2. Lest like lions they tear my throat:
    lest they carry me off and none can save me.

3. O Lord my God, if I have done such a thing:
    if there is any wickedness on my hands,

4. If I have repaid with evil him that was my friend:
    or plundered my enemy without just cause,

5. Then let the enemy pursue me and overtake me:
    let him trample my life to the ground,
  and lay my honour in the dust.

6. Arise, O Lord, in your anger:
    rise up in wrath against my adversaries.

7. Awake, my God, you that ordain justice:
    and let the assembly of the peoples gather about you;

8. Take your seat high above them:
    and sit in judgement, O Lord, over the nations.

9. Judge for me, O Lord, according to my righteousness:
    and as my integrity requires.

10. Let the wickedness of the ungodly cease,
    but establish the righteous:
    for you try the very hearts and minds of men,
    O righteous God.

11. God is my shield over me:
    he preserves the true of heart.

12. God is a righteous judge:
    and God condemns evil every day.

13. If a man does not turn, he whets his sword:
    he bends his bow and makes it ready;

14. He prepares the instruments of death:
    and makes his arrows darts of fire.

15. See how the ungodly conceives mischief:
    how he swells with wickedness and gives birth to lies.

16. He digs a pit and hollows it out:
    but falls himself into the trap he had made for others.

17. His mischief rebounds upon his own head:
    and his violence comes down on his own pate.

18. I will thank the Lord for his justice:
    I will sing praises to the Lord Most High.

Psalm 8

1. O Lord our Governor:
   how glorious is your name in all the earth!

2. Your majesty above the heavens is yet recounted:
   by the mouths of babes and sucklings.

3. You have founded a strong defence against your adversaries:
   to quell the enemy and the avenger.

4. When I consider your heavens, the work of your fingers:
   the moon and the stars which you have set in order,

5. What is man, that you should be mindful of him:
   or the son of man, that you should care for him?

6. Yet you have made him little less than a god:
    and have crowned him with glory and honour.

7. You have made him the master of your handiwork:
    and have put all things in subjection beneath his feet,

8. All sheep and oxen:
    and all the creatures of the field,

9. The birds of the air and the fish of the sea:
    and everything that moves in the pathways of the great waters.

10. O Lord our Governor:
    how glorious is your name in all the earth!

Psalm 9

1. I will give you thanks, O Lord, with my whole heart:
    I will tell of all the wonders you have done.

2. I will rejoice and be glad in you:
    I will make my songs to your name, O Most High.

3. For my enemies are driven back:
    they stumble and perish at your presence.

4. You have maintained my cause and my right:
    you sat enthroned as a righteous judge.

5. You rebuked the heathen nations,
      you brought the wicked to destruction:
    you blotted out their name for ever and ever.

6. The strongholds of the enemy are made a perpetual desolation:
    you plucked up their cities, and even their memory has perished.

7. The Lord confounds them; but the Lord endures for ever:
    he has set up his throne for judgement.

8. He shall judge the world with righteousness:
    and deal true justice to the peoples.

9. The Lord is a strong tower to him that is oppressed:
    he is a tower of strength in time of need.

10. All who heed your name will trust in you:
    for you have never forsaken those that seek you.

11. O sing praises to the Lord who dwells in Zion:
    tell among the peoples what great things he has done.

12. For he that avenges blood has remembered the poor:
    he has not forgotten their cry.

13. The Lord has been merciful toward me,
      he saw what I suffered from my foes:
    he raised me up again from the gates of death,

14. That I might tell all your praises in the gates of Zion:
    that I might rejoice in your deliverance.

15. The nations have sunk into the pit they dug for others:
    in the very snare they laid is their foot taken;

16. The Lord has declared himself and upheld the right:
    the wicked are trapped in the work of their own hands.

17. The wicked shall be given over to death:
    and all the nations that forget God.

18. For the needy shall not always be forgotten:
    nor shall the hope of the poor perish for ever.

19. Arise, Lord, let not man prevail:
    let the nations be judged before you.

20. Put them in fear, O Lord:
    and let the nations know that they are but men.

Psalm 10

1. Why do you stand far off, O Lord:
   why do you hide your face in time of need?

2. The ungodly in their pride persecute the poor:
   let them be caught in the schemes they have devised.

3. For the ungodly man boasts of his heart's desire:
   he grasps at profit, he spurns and blasphemes the Lord.

4. He says in his arrogance 'God will not avenge:'
    'There is no God' is all his thought.

5. He is settled in all his ways:
    your statutes, O Lord, are far above him,
    and he does not see.

6. He snorts defiance at his enemies, he says in his heart
    'I shall never be shaken:
    I shall walk secure from any man's curse.'

7. His mouth is full of oppression and deceit:
    mischief and wickedness lie under his tongue.

8. He skulks about in the villages:
    and secretly murders the innocent.

9. His eyes watch out for the helpless:
    he lurks concealed like a lion in a thicket.

10. He lies in wait to seize upon the poor:
    he lays hold on the poor man and drags him off in his net.

11. The upright are crushed and humbled before him:
    and the helpless fall into his power.

12. He says in his heart 'God has forgotten:
    he has covered his face and sees nothing.'

13. Arise, O Lord God, lift up your hand:
    forget not the poor for ever.

14. Why should the wicked man spurn God:
    why should he say in his heart 'He will not avenge'?

15. Surely you see the trouble and the sorrow:
    you look on, and will take it into your own hands.

16. The helpless commits himself to you:
    for you are the helper of the fatherless.

17. Break the power of the ungodly:
    search out his wickedness till it is found no more.

18. The Lord is king for ever and ever:
    the heathen have perished from his land.

19. You have heard the longing of the meek, O Lord:
    you turned your ear to their hearts' desire,

20. To help the poor and fatherless to their right:
    that men may no more be terrified from their land.

Psalm 11

1. In the Lord I have found my refuge:
   how then can you say to me
   'Flee like a bird to the mountains;

2. 'Look how the wicked bend their bows,
   and notch the arrow upon the string:
   to shoot from the darkness at the true of heart;

3. 'If the foundations are destroyed:
   what can the just man do?'

4. The Lord is in his holy place,
   the Lord is enthroned in heaven:
   his eyes search out, his glance tries the children of men.

5. He tries the righteous and the wicked:
   and him that delights in violence his soul abhors.

6. He will rain down coals of fire and brimstone
   upon the wicked:
   a scorching wind shall be their cup to drink.

7. For the Lord is righteous and loves righteous acts:
   the upright shall see his face.

Psalm 12

1. Help, Lord, for there is not one godly man left:
   the faithful have vanished from among the children of men.

2. Everyone tells lies to his neighbour:
   they flatter with their lips, but speak from a double heart.

3. If only the Lord would cut off all flattering lips:
   and the tongue that speaks so proudly!

   4. They say 'By our tongues we shall prevail:
       our lips are our servants—who is lord over us?'

   5. Because of the oppression of the poor,
       because of the groaning of the needy:
   'I will arise', says the Lord,
       'and set them in safety from those that snarl after them.'

   6. The words of the Lord are pure, as silver refined in a crucible:
       as gold that is seven times purified in the fire.

   7. You will surely guard us, O Lord:
       and shield us for ever from this evil generation,

   8. Though the ungodly strut on every side:
       though the vilest of men have mastery of mankind.

Psalm 13

   1. How long, O Lord, will you so utterly forget me:
       how long will you hide your face from me?

   2. How long must I suffer anguish in my soul,
       and be so grieved in my heart day and night:
      how long shall my enemy triumph over me?

   3. Look upon me, O Lord my God, and answer me:
       lighten my eyes, lest I sleep in death;

   4. Lest my enemy say 'I have prevailed against him':
       lest my foes exult at my overthrow.

   5. Yet I put my trust in your unfailing love:
       O let my heart rejoice in your salvation.

   6. And I will make my song to the Lord:
       because he deals so bountifully with me.

Psalm 14

   1. The fool has said in his heart 'There is no God':
       they have all become vile and abominable
     in their doings, there is not one that does good.

2. The Lord looked down from heaven
     upon the children of men:
   to see if there were any who would act wisely
     and seek after God.

3. But they have all turned out of the way,
     they have all alike become corrupt:
   there is none that does good, no not one.

4. Are all the evildoers devoid of understanding:
     who eat up my people as men eat bread,
   and do not pray to the Lord?

5. They shall be struck with terror:
     for God is with the company of the righteous.

6. Though they frustrate the poor man in his hopes:
     surely the Lord is his refuge.

7. O that deliverance for Israel might come forth
     from Zion:
   when the Lord turns again the fortunes of his people,
     then shall Jacob rejoice and Israel be glad.

Psalm 15

1. Lord, who may abide in your tabernacle:
     or who may dwell upon your holy hill?

2. He that leads an uncorrupt life
     and does the thing which is right:
   who speaks the truth from his heart,
     and has not slandered with his tongue;

3. He that has done no evil to his fellow:
     nor vented abuse against his neighbour;

4. In whose eyes the worthless have no honour:
     but he makes much of those that fear the Lord;

5. He that has sworn to his neighbour:
     and will not go back on his oath;

6. He that has not put his money to usury:
     nor taken a bribe against the innocent.

7. He that does these things:
    shall never be overthrown.

Psalm 16

1. Preserve me, O God:
    for in you have I taken refuge.

2. I have said to the Lord, You are my lord:
    and all my good depends on you.

3. As for those who are held holy on the earth:
    the other gods in whom men delight,

4. Though the idols are many that men run after:
    their offerings of blood I will not offer,
  nor take their name upon my lips.

5. The Lord is my appointed portion and my cup:
    you hold my lot in your hands.

6. The share that has fallen to me is in pleasant places:
    and a fair land is my possession.

7. I will bless the Lord who has given me counsel:
    at night also he has instructed my heart.

8. I have set the Lord always before me:
    he is at my right hand, and I shall not fall.

9. Therefore my heart is glad and my spirit rejoices:
    my flesh also shall rest secure.

10. For you will not give me over to the power of death:
    nor suffer your faithful one to see the Pit.

11. You will show me the path of life:
    in your presence is the fulness of joy,
  and from your right hand flow delights for evermore.

Psalm 17

1. Hear my just cause, O Lord, give heed to my cry:
    listen to my prayer, that comes from no lying lips.

2. Let judgement for me come forth from your presence:
   and let your eyes discern the right.

3. Though you search my heart,
    and visit me in the night-time:
 though you try me by fire,
    you will find no wickedness in me.

4. My mouth does not transgress, like the mouth of others:
   for I have kept the word of your lips.

5. My steps have held firm in the way of your commands:
   and my feet have not stumbled from your paths.

6. I call upon you, O God, for you will surely answer:
   incline your ear to me, and hear my words.

7. Show me the wonders of your steadfast love,
    O saviour of those who come to you for refuge:
 who by your right hand deliver them
    from those that rise up against them.

8. Keep me as the apple of your eye:
   hide me under the shadow of your wings,

9. From the onslaught of the wicked:
   from my enemies that encircle me to take my life.

10. They have closed their hearts to pity:
    and their mouths speak proud things.

11. They advance upon me, they surround me on every side:
    watching how they may bring me to the ground,

12. Like a lion that is greedy for its prey:
    like a lion's whelp lurking in hidden places.

13. Arise, O Lord, stand in their way and cast them down:
    deliver me from the wicked by your sword.

14. Slay them by your hand, O Lord, slay them,
    so that they perish from the earth:
 destroy them from among the living.]

15. But as for your cherished ones, let their bellies be filled
    and let their sons be satisfied:
 let them pass on their wealth to their children.

16. And I also shall see your face, because my cause is just:
    when I awake and see you as you are, I shall be satisfied.

Psalm 18

1. I love you, O Lord my strength:
   O Lord my crag, my fortress and my deliverer,

2. My God, the rock to which I come for refuge:
   my shield, my mighty saviour, and my high defence.

3. I called to the Lord with loud lamentation:
   and I was rescued from my enemies.

4. The waves of death encompassed me:
   and the floods of chaos overwhelmed me;

5. The cords of the grave tightened about me:
   and the snares of death lay in my path.

6. In my anguish I called to the Lord:
   I cried for help to my God.

7. From his temple he heard my voice:
   and my cry came even to his ears.

8. The earth heaved and quaked,
   the foundations of the hills were shaken:
   they trembled because he was angry.

9. Smoke went out from his nostrils:
   and a consuming fire from his mouth.

10. He parted the heavens and came down:
    and there was darkness under his feet.

11. He rode upon the cherubim and flew:
    he came swooping upon the wings of the wind.

12. He made the darkness his covering:
    and his canopy was thick cloud and watery darkness.

13. Out of his clouds, from the brightness before him:
    broke hailstones and coals of fire.

14. The Lord thundered in the heavens:
    the Most High uttered his voice.

15. He let loose his arrows, he scattered them on every side:
    he hurled down lightnings with the roar of the thunderbolt.

16. The springs of the sea were uncovered:
    and the foundations of the world laid bare,

17. At your rebuke, O Lord:
    at the blast of the breath of your displeasure.

18. He reached down from on high and took me:
    he drew me out of the great waters.

19. He delivered me from my strongest enemy:
    from my foes that were mightier than I.

20. They confronted me in the day of my calamity:
    but the Lord was my upholder.

21. He brought me out into a place of liberty:
    and rescued me because I delighted his heart.

22. The Lord rewarded me for my righteous dealing:
    he recompensed me according to the cleanness of my hands,

23. Because I had kept to the ways of the Lord:
    and had not turned from my God to do evil.

24. For I had an eye to all his laws:
    and did not put his commandments from me.

25. I was also blameless before him:
    and I kept myself from wrongdoing.

26. Therefore the Lord rewarded my innocence:
    because my hands were undefiled in his sight.

27. With the faithful you show yourself faithful:
    with the blameless you show yourself blameless;

28. With the pure you are pure:
    but with the crooked you show yourself perverse.

29. For you will save a humble people:
    but you bring down the high looks of the proud.

30. You light my lamp, O Lord my God:
    you make my darkness to be bright.

31. For with your help I can charge a troop of men:
    with the help of my God I can leap a city wall.

32. The way of our God is perfect,
        the word of the Lord has been tried in the fire:
    he is a shield to all that trust in him.

33. For who is God but the Lord:
        or who is our rock but our God?

34. It is God that girded me with strength:
        that made my way perfect.

35. He made my feet like the feet of a hind:
        and set me surefooted upon the mountains.

36. He taught my hands to fight:
        and my arms to aim an arrow of bronze.

37. You gave me the shield of your salvation:
        your right hand upheld me,
    and your swift response has made me great.

38. You lengthened my stride beneath me:
        and my ankles did not slip.

39. I pursued my enemies and overtook them:
        nor did I turn again till I had made an end of them.

40. I smote them, till they could rise no more:
        and they fell beneath my feet.

41. You girded me with strength for the battle:
        you threw down my adversaries under me.

42. You caused my enemies to show their backs:
        and I destroyed those that hated me.

43. They cried for help, but there was none to save them:
        they cried to the Lord, but he would not answer.

44. I pounded them fine as dust before the wind:
        I trod them under like the mire of the streets.

45. You delivered me from the strife of the peoples,
        you made me the head of the nations:
    a people that I had not known became my servants.

46. As soon as they heard me they obeyed me:
    and aliens humbled themselves before me.

47. The strength of the aliens withered away:
    they came faltering from their strongholds.

48. The Lord lives, and blessed be my rock:
    exalted be the God of my salvation,

49. The God who sees to it that I am avenged:
    who subdues the peoples under me.

50. You set me free from my enemies,
        you put me out of reach of my attackers:
    you delivered me from violent men.

51. For this will I give you thanks among the nations, O Lord:
    and sing praises to your name,

52. To him that gives great triumphs to his king:
        that deals so faithfully with his anointed;
    with David and with his seed for ever.

Psalm 19

1. The heavens declare the glory of God:
   and the firmament proclaims his handiwork;

2. One day tells it to another:
   and night to night communicates knowledge.

3. There is no speech or language:
   nor are their voices heard;

4. Yet their sound has gone out through all the world:
   and their words to the ends of the earth.

5. There he has pitched a tent for the sun:
       which comes out as a bridegroom from his chamber,
   and rejoices like a strong man to run his course.

6. Its rising is at one end of the heavens,
       And its circuit to their farthest bound:
   and nothing is hidden from its heat.

7. The law of the Lord is perfect, reviving the soul:
    the command of the Lord is true,
  and makes wise the simple.

8. The precepts of the Lord are right,
      and rejoice the heart:
    the commandment of the Lord is pure,
      and gives light to the eyes.

9. The fear of the Lord is clean, and endures for ever:
      the judgements of the Lord are unchanging,
    and righteous every one.

10. More to be desired are they than gold,
      even much fine gold:
    sweeter also than honey,
      than the honey that drips from the comb.

11. Moreover, by them is your servant taught:
      and in keeping them there is great reward.

12. Who can know his own unwitting sins?:
      O cleanse me from my secret faults.

13. Keep your servant also from presumptuous sins,
      lest they get the mastery over me:
    so I shall be clean, and innocent of great offence.

14. May the words of my mouth and the meditation
      of my heart be acceptable in your sight:
    O Lord, my strength and my redeemer.

Psalm 20

1. May the Lord hear you in the day of trouble:
     the God of Jacob lift you up to safety.

2. May he send you his help from the sanctuary:
     and be your strong support from Zion.

3. May he remember all your offerings:
     and accept with favour your burnt sacrifices,

4. Grant you your heart's desire:
     and fulfil all your purposes.

5. May we also rejoice in your victory
    and triumph in the name of our God:
  the Lord perform all your petitions.

6. Now I know that the Lord will save his anointed:
    that he will answer him from his holy heaven
  with the victorious strength of his right hand.

7. Some put their trust in chariots and some in horses:
    but we will trust in the name of the Lord our God.

8. They are brought down and fallen:
    but we're made strong and stand upright.

9. O Lord, save the king:
    and hear us when we call upon you.

Psalm 21

1. The king shall rejoice in your strength, O Lord:
    he shall exult in your salvation.

2. You have given him his heart's desire:
    you have not denied him the request of his lips.

3. For you came to meet him with the blessings of success:
    and placed a crown of gold upon his head.

4. He asked you for life and you gave it him:
    length of days for ever and ever.

5. Great is his glory because of your salvation:
    you have clothed him with honour and majesty.

6. You have given him everlasting felicity:
    and made him glad with the joy of your presence.

7. For the king puts his trust in the Lord:
    and through the tender mercy of the Most High
  he shall never be moved.

8. Your hand shall light upon your enemies:
    and your right hand shall find out all who hate you.

9. You will make them like a blazing furnace
    in the day of your coming:

       the Lord will overwhelm them in his wrath,
          and fire shall consume them.

10. You will root out their offspring from the earth:
       and their seed from among the children of men;

11. Because they have stirred up evil against you:
       and plotted mischief, which they cannot perform.

12. Therefore will you set your shoulder toward them:
       and draw the string of the bow to strike at their faces.

13. Arise, O Lord, in your great strength:
       and we will sing and praise your power.

Psalm 22

1. My God, my God, why have you forsaken me:
       why are you so far from helping me
   and from the words of my groaning?

2. My God, I cry to you by day, but you do not answer:
       and by night also I take no rest.

3. But you continue holy:
       you that are the praise of Israel.

4. In you our fathers trusted:
       they trusted, and you delivered them;

5. To you they cried and they were saved:
       they put their trust in you and were not confounded.

6. But as for me, I am a worm and no man:
       the scorn of men and despised by the people.

7. All those that see me laugh me to scorn:
       they shoot out their lips at me and wag their heads,
   saying,

8. 'He trusted in the Lord—let him deliver him:
       let him deliver him, if he delights in him.'

9. But you are he that took me out of the womb:
       that brought me to lie at peace on my mother's breast.

10. On you have I been cast since my birth:
    you are my God, even from my mother's womb.

11. O go not from me, for trouble is hard at hand:
    and there is none to help.

12. Many oxen surround me:
    fat bulls of Bashan close me in on every side.

13. They gape wide their mouths at me:
    like lions that roar and rend.

14. I am poured out like water,
    and all my bones are out of joint:
    my heart within my breast is like melting wax.

15. My mouth is dried up like a potsherd:
    and my tongue clings to my gums.

16. My hands and my feet are withered:
    and you lay me in the dust of death.

17. For many dogs are come about me:
    and a band of evildoers hem me in.

18. I can count all my bones:
    they stand staring and gazing upon me.

19. They part my garments among them:
    and cast lots for my clothing.

20. O Lord, do not stand far off:
    you are my helper, hasten to my aid.

21. Deliver my body from the sword:
    my life from the power of the dogs;

22. O save me from the lion's mouth:
    and my afflicted soul from the horns of the wild oxen.

23. I will tell of your name to my brethren:
    in the midst of the congregation will I praise you.

24. O praise the Lord, all you that fear him:
    hold him in honour, O seed of Jacob,
    and let the seed of Israel stand in awe of him.

25. For he has not despised nor abhorred
     the poor man in his misery:
 nor did he hide his face from him,
     but heard him when he cried.

26. From you springs my praise in the great congregation:
     I will pay my vows in the sight of all that fear you;

27. The meek shall eat of the sacrifice and be satisfied:
     and those who seek the Lord shall praise him—
 may their hearts rejoice for ever!

28. Let all the ends of the earth remember
     and turn to the Lord:
 and let all the families of the nations worship before him.

29. For the kingdom is the Lord's:
     and he shall be ruler over the nations.

30. How can those who sleep in the earth do him homage:
     or those that descend to the dust bow down before him?

31. But he has saved my life for himself:
     and my posterity shall serve him.

32. This shall be told of my Lord to a future generation:
     and his righteousness declared to a people yet unborn,
 that he has done it.

Psalm 23

1. The Lord is my shepherd:
     therefore can I lack nothing.

2. He will make me lie down in green pastures:
     and lead me beside still waters.

3. He will refresh my soul:
     and guide me in right pathways for his name's sake.

4. Though I walk through the valley of the shadow of death,
     I will fear no evil:
 for you are with me, your rod and your staff comfort me.

5. You spread a table before me
       in the face of those who trouble me:
   you have anointed my head with oil,
       and my cup will be full.

6. Surely your goodness and loving-kindness
       will follow me all the days of my life:
   and I shall dwell in the house of the Lord for ever.

Psalm 24

1. The earth is the Lord's and all that is in it:
       the compass of the world and those who dwell therein.

2. For he has founded it upon the seas:
       and established it upon the waters.

3. Who shall ascend the hill of the Lord:
       or who shall stand in his holy place?

4. He that has clean hands and a pure heart:
       who has not set his soul upon idols,
   nor sworn his oath to a lie.

5. He shall receive blessing from the Lord:
       and recompense from the God of his salvation.

6. Of such a kind as this are those who seek him:
       those who seek your face, O God of Jacob.

7. Lift up your heads, O you gates,
       and be lifted up, you everlasting doors:
   and the King of glory shall come in.

8. Who is the King of glory?:
       the Lord, strong and mighty,
   the Lord mighty in battle.

9. Lift up your heads, O you gates,
       and be lifted up, you everlasting doors:
   and the King of glory shall come in.

10. Who is the King of glory?:
        the Lord of hosts, he is the King of glory.

Psalm 25

1. In you, O Lord my God, have I put my hope:
    in you have I trusted, let me not be ashamed,
   nor let my enemies triumph over me.

2. Let none who wait for you be put to shame:
    but let those that break faith
   be confounded and gain nothing.

3. Show me your ways, O Lord:
    and teach me your paths.

4. Lead me in the ways of your truth, and teach me:
    for you are the God of my salvation.

5. In you have I hoped all the day long:
    because of your goodness, O Lord.

6. Call to mind your compassion and your loving-kindness:
    for they are from of old.

7. Remember not the sins of my youth,
    nor my transgressions:
   but according to your mercy think on me.

8. Good and upright is the Lord:
    therefore will he direct sinners in the way.

9. The meek he will guide in the path of justice:
    and teach the humble his ways.

10. All the paths of the Lord are faithful and true:
    for those who keep his covenant and his commandments.

11. For your name's sake, O Lord:
    be merciful to my sin, though it is great.

12. Who is he that fears the Lord?:
    him will the Lord direct in the way that he should choose.

13. His soul shall dwell at ease:
    and his children shall inherit the land.

14. The confidences of God belong to those that fear him:
    and his covenant shall give them understanding.

15. My eyes are ever looking to the Lord:
    for he will bring my feet out of the net.
16. Turn your face toward me and be gracious:
    for I am alone and in misery.
17. O free my heart from pain:
    and bring me out of my distress.
18. Give heed to my affliction and adversity:
    and forgive me all my sins.
19. Consider my enemies, how many they are:
    and they bear a violent hate against me.
20. O keep my life, and deliver me:
    put me not to shame, for I come to you for refuge.
21. Let innocence and integrity be my guard:
    for in you have I hoped.
22. O God, deliver Israel:
    out of all his tribulation.

Psalm 26

1. Give judgement for me, O Lord,
       for I have walked in my integrity:
    I have trusted in the Lord and not wavered.
2. Put me to the test, O Lord, and prove me:
    try my mind and my heart.
3. For your steadfast love has been ever before my eyes:
    and I have walked in your truth.
4. I have not sat with deceivers:
    nor consorted with the hypocrites;
5. I hate the assembly of the wicked:
    I will not sit with the ungodly.
6. I wash my hands in innocence, O Lord:
    that I may go about your altar,
7. And lift up the voice of thanksgiving:
    to tell of all your marvellous works.

8. Lord, I love the house of your habitation:
    and the place where your glory dwells.

9. Do not sweep me away with sinners:
    nor my life with men of blood,

10. In whose hand is abomination:
    and their right hand is full of bribes.

11. As for me, I walk in my integrity:
    O ransom me and be favourable toward me.

12. My foot stands on an even path:
    I will bless the Lord in the great congregation.

Psalm 27

1. The Lord is my light and my salvation;
    whom then shall I fear?:
    the Lord is the stronghold of my life;
    of whom shall I be afraid?

2. When the wicked, even my enemies and my foes,
    come upon me to devour me:
    they shall stumble and fall.

3. If an army encamp against me,
    my heart shall not be afraid:
    and if war should rise against me, yet will I trust.

4. One thing I have asked from the Lord,
    which I will require:
    that I may dwell in the house of the Lord
    all the days of my life,

5. To see the fair beauty of the Lord:
    and to seek his will in his temple.

6. For he will hide me under his shelter in the day of trouble:
    and conceal me in the shadow of his tent,
    and set me high upon a rock.

7. And now he will lift up my head:
    above my enemies round about me.

8. And I will offer sacrifices in his sanctuary
    with exultation:
  I will sing, I will sing praises to the Lord.

9. O Lord, hear my voice when I cry:
  have mercy upon me and answer me.

10. My heart has said of you, 'Seek his face':
  your face, Lord, I will seek.

11. Do not hide your face from me:
  or thrust your servant aside in displeasure;

12. For you have been my helper:
    do not cast me away or forsake me,
  O God of my salvation.

13. Though my father and my mother forsake me:
  the Lord will take me up.

14. Teach me your way, O Lord:
    and lead me in an even path,
  for they lie in wait for me.

15. Do not give me over to the will of my enemies:
    for false witnesses have risen against me,
  and those who breathe out violence.

16. But I believe that I shall surely see
    the goodness of the Lord:
  in the land of the living.

17. O wait for the Lord;
    stand firm and he will strengthen your heart:
  and wait, I say, for the Lord.

Psalm 28

1. To you will I cry, O Lord my Rock,
    be not deaf to my prayer:
  lest, if you turn away silent,
    I become like those that go down to the grave.

2. Hear the voice of my supplication
    when I cry to you for help:

      when I lift up my hands
          toward the holiest place of your sanctuary.

3. Do not snatch me away with the ungodly,
      with the evildoers:
  who speak peace to their neighbours,
      but nourish malice in their hearts.

4. Repay them according to their deeds:
      and according to the wickedness of their endeavours;

5. Requite them for the work of their hands:
      and give them their deserts.

6. For they pay no heed to the Lord's acts,
      nor to the operation of his hands:
  therefore shall he break them down
      and not build them up.

7. Let the Lord's name be praised:
      for he has heard the voice of my supplication.

8. The Lord is my strength and my shield,
      in him my heart trusts and I am helped:
  therefore my heart dances for joy,
      and in my song will I praise him.

9. The Lord is the strength of his people:
      and a sure refuge for his anointed king.

10. O save your people and give your blessing to your own:
      be their shepherd, and bear them up for ever.

Psalm 29

1. Ascribe to the Lord, you sons of heaven:
      ascribe to the Lord glory and might.

2. Ascribe to the Lord the honour due to his name:
      O worship the Lord in the beauty of his holiness.

3. The voice of the Lord is upon the waters:
      the God of glory thunders,
  the Lord upon the great waters.

4. The voice of the Lord is mighty in operation:
    the voice of the Lord is a glorious voice.

5. The voice of the Lord breaks the cedar-trees:
    the Lord breaks in pieces the cedars of Lebanon.

6. He makes them skip like a calf:
    Lebanon and Sirion like a young wild ox.

7. The voice of the Lord divides the lightning-flash:
    the voice of the Lord whirls the sands of the desert,
  the Lord whirls the desert of Kadesh.

8. The voice of the Lord rends the terebinth trees,
        and strips bare the forests:
  in his temple all cry 'Glory'.

9. The Lord sits enthroned above the water-flood:
    the Lord sits enthroned as a king for ever.

10. The Lord will give strength to his people:
    the Lord will give to his people the blessing of peace.

Psalm 30

1. I will exalt you, O Lord,
        for you have drawn me up from the depths:
    and have not suffered my foes to triumph over me.

2. O Lord my God, I cried to you:
    and you have made me whole.

3. You brought me back, O Lord, from the land of silence:
        you saved my life
    from among those that go down to the Pit.

4. Sing praises to the Lord, all you his faithful ones:
    and give thanks to his holy name.

5. For if in his anger is havoc,
        in his good favour is life:
    heaviness may endure for a night,
        but joy comes in the morning.

6. In my prosperity I said 'I shall never be moved:
    your goodness, O Lord, has set me on so firm a hill.'

7. Then you hid your face from me:
   　　and I was greatly dismayed.

8. I cried to you, O God:
   　　and made my petition humbly to my Lord.

9. 'What profit is there in my blood,
   　　if I go down to the Pit:
   can the dust give you thanks,
   　　or declare your faithfulness?

10. 'Hear, O Lord, and be merciful:
    　　O Lord, be my helper.'

11. You have turned my lamentation into dancing:
    　　you have put off my sackcloth and girded me with joy,

12. That my heart may sing your praise and never be silent:
    　　O Lord my God, I will give you thanks for ever.

Psalm 31

1. To you, Lord, have I come for shelter:
   　　let me never be put to shame.

2. O deliver me in your righteousness:
   　　incline your ear to me and be swift to save me.

3. Be for me a rock of refuge, a fortress to defend me:
   　　for you are my high rock and my stronghold.

4. Lead me and guide me for your name's sake:
   　　bring me out of the net that they have secretly laid for me,
   for you are my strength.

5. Into your hands I commit my spirit:
   　　you will redeem me, O Lord God of truth.

6. I hate those that clutch vain idols:
   　　but my trust is in the Lord.

7. I will rejoice and be glad in your loving-kindness:
   　　for you have looked on my distress
   and known me in adversity.

8. You have not given me over to the power of the enemy:
    you have set my feet where I may walk at liberty.

9. Have mercy upon me, O Lord, for I am in trouble:
    my eye wastes away for grief,
   my throat also and my inward parts.

10. For my life wears out in sorrow,
      and my years with sighing:
    my strength fails me in my affliction,
      and my bones are consumed.

11. I am become the scorn of all my enemies:
    and my neighbours wag their heads in derision.

12. I am a thing of horror to my friends:
    and those that see me in the street shrink from me.

13. I am forgotten like a dead man out of mind:
    I have become like a broken vessel.

14. For I hear the whispering of many:
    and fear is on every side;

15. While they plot together against me:
    and scheme to take away my life.

16. But in you, Lord, have I put my trust:
    I have said 'You are my God'.

17. All my days are in your hand:
    O deliver me from the power of my enemies
    and from my persecutors.

18. Make your face to shine upon your servant:
    and save me for your mercy's sake.

19. O Lord, let me not be confounded,
      for I have called upon you:
    but let the wicked be put to shame
      and brought to silence in the grave.

20. Let the lying lips be dumb:
      that in pride and contempt
    speak such insolence against the just.

21. O how plentiful is your goodness,
	stored up for those that fear you:
   and prepared in the sight of men
	for all who come to you for refuge.

22. You will hide them in the cover of your presence
	from the plots of men:
   you will shelter them in your refuge
	from the strife of tongues.

23. Blessed be the Lord our God:
	for he has wonderfully shown me his steadfast love,
   when I was as a city besieged.

24. When I was afraid, I said in my haste:
	'I am cut off from your sight'.

25. But you heard the voice of my supplication:
	when I cried to you for help.

26. Love the Lord, all you his faithful ones:
	for the Lord guards the true,
   but fully requites the proud.

27. Be strong, and let your heart take courage:
	all you that hope in the Lord.

Psalm 32

1. Blessed is he whose sin is forgiven:
	whose iniquity is put away.

2. Blessed is the man to whom the Lord imputes no blame:
	and in whose spirit there is no guile.

3. For whilst I held my tongue:
	my bones wasted away with my daily complaining.

4. Your hand was heavy upon me day and night:
	and my moisture was dried up like a drought in summer.

5. Then I acknowledged my sin to you:
	and my iniquity I did not hide;

6. I said 'I will confess my transgressions to the Lord':
    and so you forgave the wickedness of my sin.

7. For this cause shall everyone that is faithful
      make his prayer to you in the day of trouble:
    and in the time of the great water-floods,
      they shall not come near him.

8. You are a place to hide me in,
      you will preserve me from trouble:
    you will surround me with deliverance on every side.

9. 'I will instruct you,
      and direct you in the way that you should go:
    I will fasten my eye upon you, and give you counsel.

10. 'Be not like horse or mule, that have no understanding:
      whose forward course must be curbed with bit and bridle.'

11. Great tribulations remain for the ungodly:
      but whoever puts his trust in the Lord,
    mercy embraces him on every side.

12. Rejoice in the Lord, you righteous, and be glad:
      and shout for joy, all you that are true of heart.

Psalm 33

1. Rejoice in the Lord, you righteous:
    for it befits the just to praise him.

2. Give the Lord thanks upon the harp:
    and sing his praise to the lute of ten strings.

3. O sing him a new song:
    make sweetest melody, with shouts of praise.

4. For the word of the Lord is true:
    and all his works are faithful.

5. He loves righteousness and justice:
    the earth is filled with the loving-kindness of the Lord.

6. By the word of the Lord were the heavens made:
    and their numberless stars by the breath of his mouth.

7. He gathered the waters of the sea as in a water-skin:
    and laid up the deep in his treasuries.

8. Let the whole earth fear the Lord:
    and let all the inhabitants of the world stand in awe of him.

9. For he spoke, and it was done:
    he commanded, and it stood fast.

10. The Lord frustrates the counsels of the nations:
    he brings to nothing the devices of the peoples.

11. But the counsels of the Lord shall endure for ever:
    the purposes of his heart from generation to generation.

12. Blessed is that nation whose God is the Lord:
    the people he chose to be his own possession.

13. The Lord looks down from heaven
    and surveys all the children of men:
    he considers from his dwelling-place
    all the inhabitants of the earth;

14. He who fashioned the hearts of them all:
    and comprehends all that they do.

15. A king is not saved by a mighty army:
    nor is a warrior delivered by much strength.

16. A horse is a vain hope to save a man:
    nor can he rescue any by his great power.

17. But the eye of the Lord is on those that fear him:
    on those that trust in his unfailing love,

18. To deliver them from death:
    and to feed them in the time of dearth.

19. We have waited eagerly for the Lord:
    for he is our help and our shield.

20. Surely our hearts shall rejoice in him:
    for we have trusted in his holy name.

21. Let your merciful kindness be upon us, O Lord:
    even as our hope is in you.

Psalm 34

1. I will bless the Lord continually:
    his praise shall be always in my mouth.
2. Let my soul boast of the Lord:
    the humble shall hear it and rejoice.
3. O praise the Lord with me:
    let us exalt his name together.
4. For I sought the Lord's help and he answered:
    and he freed me from all my fears.
5. Look towards him and be bright with joy:
    your faces shall not be ashamed.
6. Here is a wretch who cried, and the Lord heard him:
    and saved him from all his troubles.
7. The angel of the Lord encamps round those who fear him:
    and delivers them in their need.
8. O taste and see that the Lord is good:
    happy the man who hides in him!
9. Fear the Lord, all you his holy ones:
    for those who fear him never lack.
10. Lions may suffer want and go hungry:
    but those who seek the Lord lack nothing good.
11. Come, my children, listen to me:
    and I will teach you the fear of the Lord.
12. Which of you relishes life:
    wants time to enjoy good things?
13. Keep your tongue from evil:
    and your lips from telling lies.
14. Turn from evil and do good:
    seek peace and pursue it.
15. The eyes of God are on the righteous:
    and his ears towards their cry.

16. The Lord sets his face against wrongdoers:
    to root out their memory from the earth.

17. The righteous cry; the Lord hears it:
    and frees them from all their afflictions.

18. The Lord is close to those who are broken-hearted:
    and the crushed in spirit he saves.

19. The trials of the righteous are many:
    but our God delivers him from them all.

20. He guards all his bones:
    so that not one is broken.

21. Evil will slay the wicked:
    and those who hate the righteous will be destroyed.

22. The Lord ransoms the lives of his servants:
    and none who hide in him will be destroyed.

Psalm 35

1. Contend, O Lord, with those who contend with me:
   fight against those that fight against me.

2. Take up shield and buckler:
   and arise, arise to help me.

3. Draw the spear
       and bar the way against those that pursue me:
   say to me 'I am your deliverer'.

4. Let those that seek my life
       be put to shame and disgraced:
   let those that plot my destruction
       be turned back and confounded.

5. Let them be like chaff before the wind:
   with the angel of the Lord driving them;

6. Let their way be dark and slippery:
   with the angel of the Lord pursuing.

7. For without cause
       they have secretly spread a net for me:
   without cause they have dug a pit to entrap me.

8. Let sudden disaster strike them:
       let the net that they have hidden catch them,
   let them fall to their destruction.

9. Then shall my soul be joyful in the Lord:
       and I will rejoice in his deliverance.

10. All my bones shall say 'Lord, who is like you?:
        for you deliver the poor man
    from him that is too strong for him,
        the poor and needy from him that would despoil them'.

11. Malicious witnesses rise up against me:
        I am questioned about things of which I know nothing.

12. They repay me evil for good:
        I am as one bereaved of his children.

13. Yet when they were sick, I put on sackcloth:
        I afflicted myself with fasting.

14. And if my prayer returned unanswered to my bosom:
        I went about mourning
    as though for a brother or a companion;

15. I was bowed down with grief:
        as though for my own mother.

16. But when I stumbled, they rejoiced and gathered together,
        they gathered together against me:
    as though they were strangers I never knew,
        they tore at me without ceasing.

17. When I slipped, they mocked me:
        and gnashed at me with their teeth.

18. Lord, how long will you look on?:
        take me from the evil they intend,
    take me from amidst the lions.

19. And I will give you thanks in the great congregation:
        I will praise you in the throng of the people.

20. Let not those that wrongfully are my enemies
        triumph over me:
    let not those that hate me without cause
        mock me with their eyes.

21. For they speak words that do not make for peace:
        they invent lies against those that are quiet in the land.

22. They stretch their mouths to jeer at me, and say:
        'Aha, aha! We have seen all that we wish!'

23. And you also have seen, O Lord; do not be silent:
        O God, go not far from me.

24. Bestir yourself, awake to do me right:
        to plead my cause, O Lord my God.

25. Judge me, O Lord my God,
        according to your righteousness:
    and let them not rejoice over me.

26. Let them not say in their hearts 'We have our wish':
        let them not say 'We have destroyed him'.

27. Let those that rejoice at my hurt
        be disgraced and confounded altogether:
    let those that lord it over me
        be clothed in shame and dishonour.

28. But let those that long for my vindication
        shout for joy and rejoice:
    let them say always that the Lord is great,
        who takes such delight in his servant's good.

29. And my tongue shall speak of your righteousness:
        and of your praise all the day long.

Psalm 36

1. The transgressor speaks from the wickedness in his own heart:
        there is no fear of God before his eyes.

2. For he flatters himself in his own sight:
        he hates his iniquity to be found out.

3. The words of his mouth are wickedness and deceit:
    he has ceased to act wisely and do good.

4. He plots mischief as he lies upon his bed:
    he has set himself on a path that is not good,
   he does not spurn evil.

5. Your unfailing kindness, O Lord, is in the heavens:
    and your faithfulness reaches to the clouds.

6. Your righteousness is like the strong mountains:
    and your justice as the great deep;
   you, O Lord, save both man and beast.

7. How precious, O God, is your enduring kindness:
    the children of men shall take refuge
   under the shadow of your wings.

8. They shall be satisfied
      with the good things of your house:
    and you will give them drink
      from the river of your delights.

9. For with you is the well of life:
    and in your light shall we see light.

10. O continue your merciful kindness
      toward those who know you:
    and your righteous dealing
      to those that are true of heart.

11. Let not the foot of the proud come against me:
    nor the hand of the ungodly drive me away.

12. There are they fallen, those who do evil:
    they are thrust down, and shall not rise again.

Psalm 37

1. Do not vie with the wicked:
    or envy those that do wrong;

2. For they will soon wither like the grass:
    and fade away like the green leaf.

The Psalms

3. Trust in the Lord and do good:
    and you shall dwell in the land
   and feed in safe pastures.

4. Let the Lord be your delight:
    and he will grant you your heart's desire.

5. Commit your way to the Lord:
    trust him, and he will act.

6. He will make your righteousness
    shine as clear as the light:
   and your innocence as the noonday.

7. Be still before the Lord, and wait patiently for him:
    do not be vexed when a man prospers,
   when he puts his evil purposes to work.

8. Let go of anger and abandon wrath:
    let not envy move you to do evil.

9. For the wicked shall be cut down:
    but those who wait for the Lord shall possess the land.

10. In a little while the ungodly shall be no more:
     you will look for him in his place,
    but he will not be found.

11. But the meek shall possess the land:
     and enjoy the abundance of peace.

12. The ungodly man plots against the righteous:
     and gnashes at him with his teeth.

13. But the Lord shall laugh him to scorn:
     for he sees that the day for his overthrow is near.

14. The ungodly have drawn the sword and strung the bow:
     to strike down the poor and needy,
    to slaughter those that walk in innocence.

15. Their swords shall pierce their own hearts:
     and their bows shall be broken.

16. Though the righteous man has but a little:
     it is better than the great wealth of the ungodly.

17. For the strong arm of the ungodly shall be broken:
    but the Lord upholds the righteous.
18. The Lord cares for the lives of the innocent:
    and their heritage shall be theirs for ever.
19. They shall not be put to shame in the evil days:
    but in time of famine they shall eat their fill.
20. As for the ungodly, they shall perish,
        they are the enemies of the Lord:
    like fuel in a furnace they shall vanish away in smoke.
21. The ungodly man borrows but does not repay:
    but the righteous is gracious, and gives.
22. Those who are blessed by God shall possess the land:
    but those whom he has cursed shall be cut down.
23. If a man's steps are guided by the Lord:
    and he delights in his way,
24. Though he stumble, he shall not fall headlong:
    for the Lord holds him by the hand.
25. I have been young and now am old:
    but I never saw the righteous man forsaken,
    or his children begging their bread.
26. He is ever gracious, and lends:
    and his children shall be blessed.
27. Turn from evil and do good:
    and you shall dwell in the land for ever.
28. For the Lord loves justice:
    he will not forsake his faithful ones.
29. But the unjust shall be destroyed for ever:
    and the children of the ungodly shall be cut down.
30. The just shall possess the land:
    and they shall dwell in it for ever.
31. The mouth of the righteous man utters wisdom:
    and his tongue speaks what is right.

32. The law of his God is in his heart:
    and his footsteps will not slip.

33. The ungodly man watches out for the righteous:
    and seeks occasion to slay him.

34. But the Lord will not abandon him to his power.
    nor let him be condemned when he is judged.

35. Wait for the Lord, and hold to his way:
    and he will raise you up to possess the land,
    to see the ungodly when they are destroyed.

36. I have seen the ungodly in terrifying power:
    spreading himself like a luxuriant tree;

37. I passed by again, and he was gone:
    I searched for him, but he could not be found.

38. Observe the blameless man and consider the upright:
    for the man of peace shall have posterity.

39. But transgressors shall be destroyed altogether:
    and the posterity of the wicked shall be cut down.

40. Deliverance for the righteous shall come from the Lord:
    he is their strength in time of trouble.

41. The Lord will help them and deliver them:
    he will save them from the ungodly and deliver them,
    because they come to him for refuge.

Psalm 38

1. O Lord, rebuke me not in your anger:
   nor chasten me in your fierce displeasure.

2. For your arrows have been aimed against me:
   and your hand has come down heavy upon me.

3. There is no health in my flesh
     because of your indignation:
   nor soundness in my bones, by reason of my sin.

4. The tide of my iniquities has gone over my head:
    their weight is a burden too heavy for me to bear.

5. My wounds stink and fester:
    because of my foolishness.

6. I am bowed down and brought so low:
    that I go mourning all the day long.

7. For my loins are filled with a burning pain:
    and there is no sound part in all my body.

8. I am numbed and stricken to the ground:
    I cry aloud in the yearning of my heart.

9. O Lord, all I long for is before you:
    and my deep sighing is not hidden from you.

10. My heart is in tumult, my strength fails me:
    and even the light of my eyes has gone from me.

11. My friends and my companions
        hold aloof from my affliction:
    and my kinsmen stand far off.

12. Those who seek my life strike at me:
    and those that desire my hurt spread evil tales,
    and murmur slanders all the day.

13. But I am like a deaf man and hear nothing:
    like one that is dumb, who does not open his mouth.

14. So I have become as one who cannot hear:
    in whose mouth there is no retort.

15. For in you, Lord, have I put my trust:
    and you will answer me, O Lord my God.

16. For I prayed 'Let them never exult over me:
    those who turn arrogant when my foot slips'.

17. Truly, I am ready to fall:
    and my pain is with me continually.

18. But I acknowledge my wickedness:
    and I am filled with sorrow at my sin.

19. Those that are my enemies without cause
     are great in number:
   and those who hate me wrongfully are many.

20. Those also who repay evil for good are against me:
     because I seek after good.

21. Forsake me not, O Lord,
     go not far from me, my God:
   hasten to my help, O Lord my salvation.

Psalm 39

1. I said 'I will keep watch over my ways,
    lest I sin with my tongue:
   I will keep a guard on my mouth
    while the wicked are in my sight.'

2. I held my tongue and said nothing:
    I kept silent, but found no comfort.

3. My pain was increased, my heart grew hot within me:
    while I mused, the fire blazed,
   and I spoke with my tongue;

4. 'Lord, let me know my end:
    and the number of my days,

5. 'That I may know how short my time is:
    for you have made my days but a handsbreadth
   and my whole span is as nothing before you.'

6. Surely every man, though he stand secure, is but breath:
    man lives as a passing shadow.

7. The riches he heaps are but a puff of wind:
    and he cannot tell who will gather them.

8. And now, Lord, what is my hope?:
    truly my hope is in you.

9. O deliver me from all my transgressions:
    do not make me the butt of fools.

10. I was dumb, I did not open my mouth:
    for surely it was your doing.

11. Take away your plague from me:
    I am brought to an end by the blows of your hand.

12. When with rebukes you chastise a man for sin:
    you cause his fair looks to dissolve in putrefaction
    —surely every man is but breath.

13. Hear my prayer, O Lord, and give ear to my cry:
    be not silent at my tears.

14. For I am but a stranger with you:
    a passing guest as all my fathers were.

15. Turn your eye from me, that I may smile again:
    before I go hence and am no more.

Psalm 40

1. I waited patiently for the Lord:
   and he inclined to me and heard my cry.

2. He brought me up from the pit of roaring waters,
       out of the mire and clay:
   and set my feet upon a rock, and made firm my foothold.

3. And he has put a new song in my mouth:
   even a song of thanksgiving to our God.

4. Many shall see it and fear:
   and shall put their trust in the Lord.

5. Blessed is the man who has made the Lord his hope:
       who has not turned to the proud,
   or to those who wander in deceit.

6. O Lord my God, great are the wonderful things which you have done,
       and your thoughts which are towards us:
   there is none to be compared with you;

7. Were I to declare them and speak of them:
   they are more than I am able to express.

8. Sacrifice and offering you do not desire:
    but my ears you have marked for obedience;
9. Burnt-offering and sin-offering you have not required:
    then said I, Lo, I come.
10. In the scroll of the book it is written of me,
     that I should do your will:
   O my God, I long to do it, your law delights my heart.
11. I have declared your righteousness
     in the great congregation:
   I have not restrained my lips, O Lord,
     and that you know.
12. I have not hidden your righteousness in my heart:
     I have spoken of your faithfulness and of your salvation.
13. I have not kept back your loving-kindness and your truth:
     from the great congregation.
14. O Lord, do not withhold your mercy from me:
     let your loving-kindness and your truth ever preserve me.
15. For innumerable troubles have come upon me:
     my sins have overtaken me, and I cannot see.
16. They are more in number than the hairs of my head:
     therefore my heart fails me.
17. Be pleased, O Lord, to deliver me:
     O Lord, make haste to help me.
18. Let those who seek my life to take it away:
     be put to shame and confounded altogether.
19. Let them be turned back and disgraced who wish me evil:
     let them be aghast for shame who say to me 'Aha, aha!'
20. Let all who seek you be joyful and glad because of you:
     let those who love your salvation say always
    'The Lord is great.'
21. As for me, I am poor and needy:
     but the Lord will care for me.
22. You are my helper and my deliverer:
     make no long delay, O Lord my God.

Psalm 41

1. Blessed is he that considers the poor and helpless:
    the Lord will deliver him in the day of trouble.

2. The Lord will guard him and preserve his life,
    he shall be counted happy in the land:
   you will not give him over to the will of his enemies.

3. And if he lies sick on his bed, the Lord will sustain him:
    if illness lays him low, you will overthrow it.

4. I said 'O Lord, be merciful toward me:
    heal me, for I have sinned against you'.

5. My enemies speak evil of me, saying:
    'When will he die, and his name perish for ever?'

6. And if one should come to see me,
    he mouths empty words:
   while his heart gathers mischief,
    and when he goes out, he vents it.

7. All those that hate me whisper together against me:
    they devise plots against me.

8. They say 'A deadly thing has got hold of him:
    he will not get up again from where he lies'.

9. Even my bosom friend in whom I trusted:
    who shared my bread, has lifted his heel against me.

10. But you, O Lord, be gracious and raise me up:
     and I will repay them what they have deserved.

11. By this will I know that you favour me:
     That my enemy shall not triumph over me.

12. Because of my innocence you hold me fast:
     you have set me before your face for ever.

13. Blessed be the Lord, the God of Israel:
     from everlasting to everlasting. Amen, amen.

Psalm 42

1. As a deer longs for the running brooks:
    so longs my soul for you, O God.

2. My soul is thirsty for God, thirsty for the living God:
    when shall I come and see his face?

3. My tears have been my food day and night:
    while they ask me all day long 'Where now is your God?'

4. As I pour out my soul by myself, I remember this:
    how I went to the house of the Mighty One,
   into the temple of God,

5. To the shouts and songs of thanksgiving:
    a multitude keeping high festival.

6. *Why are you so full of heaviness, my soul:*
    and why so unquiet within me?

7. *O put your trust in God:*
    for I will praise him yet, who is my deliverer and my God.

8. My soul is heavy within me:
    therefore I will remember you from the land of Jordan,
   from Mizar among the hills of Hermon.

9. Deep calls to deep in the roar of your waters:
    all your waves and breakers have gone over me.

10. Surely the Lord will grant his loving mercy
     in the day-time:
    and in the night his song will be with me,
     a prayer to the God of my life.

11. I will say to God, my rock, 'Why have you forgotten me:
     why must I go like a mourner
    because the enemy oppresses me?'

12. Like a sword through my bones, my enemies have mocked me:
     while they ask me all day long 'Where now is your God?'

13. *Why are you so full of heaviness, my soul:*
     and why so unquiet within me?

14. *O put your trust in God:*
    for I will praise him yet, who is my deliverer and my God.

Psalm 43

1. Give judgement for me, O God,
       take up my cause against an ungodly people:
   deliver me from deceitful and wicked men.

2. For you are God my refuge—
       why have you turned me away?:
   why must I go like a mourner
       because the enemy oppresses me?

3. O send out your light and your truth,
       and let them lead me:
   let them guide me to your holy hill and to your dwelling.

4. Then I shall go to the altar of God,
       to God my joy and my delight:
   and to the harp I shall sing your praises, O God, my God.

5. *Why are you so full of heaviness, my soul:*
       and why so unquiet within me?

6. *O put your trust in God:*
       for I will praise him yet, who is my deliverer and my God.

Psalm 44

1. We have heard with our ears, O God,
       our fathers have told us:
   what things you did in their time, in the days of old;

2. How by your own hand you drove out the nations,
       and planted us in:
   how you crushed the peoples,
       but caused us to root and grow.

3. For it was not by their swords
       that our fathers took possession of the land:
   nor did their own arm get them the victory,

4. But your right hand, your arm,
    and the light of your countenance:
because you delighted in them.

5. You are my king and my God:
    who ordained victory for Jacob.

6. By your power we struck our enemies through:
    in your name we trod down those that rose against us.

7. For I did not trust in my bow:
    nor could my sword save me;

8. But it was you that delivered us from our enemies:
    and put our adversaries to confusion.

9. In God we made our boast all the day long:
    we gave thanks to your name without ceasing.

10. But now you have cast us off and brought us to shame:
    you go not out with our armies.

11. You have caused us to show our backs to the enemy:
    so that our foes plunder us at will.

12. You have given us like sheep to be butchered:
    you have scattered us among the nations.

13. You have sold your people for nothing:
    and made a profitless bargain.

14. You have made us a laughing-stock to our neighbours:
    mocked and held in derision by those about us.

15. You have made us a byword among the nations:
    so that the peoples toss their heads in scorn.

16. My disgrace is before me all the day:
    and shame has covered my face,

17. At the voice of the slanderer and reviler:
    at the sight of the enemy and avenger.

18. All this has come upon us,
    though we have not forgotten you:
we have not betrayed your covenant.

19. Our hearts have not turned back:
    nor have our steps strayed from your paths.

20. And yet you have crushed us in the haunt of jackals:
    and covered us with the shadow of death.

21. If we had forgotten the name of our God:
    or stretched out our hands in prayer to some strange god,

22. Would not God search it out?:
    for he knows the very secrets of the heart.

23. But for your sake are we killed all the day long:
    we are counted as sheep for the slaughter.

24. Rouse yourself, O Lord, why do you sleep?:
    awake, do not cast us off for ever.

25. Why do you hide your face:
    and forget our misery and our affliction?

26. Our souls are bowed to the dust:
    our bellies cleave to the ground.

27. Arise, O Lord, to help us:
    and redeem us for your mercy's sake.

Psalm 45

1. My heart is astir with fine phrases,
        I make my song for a king:
    my tongue is the pen of a ready writer.

2. You are the fairest of the sons of men,
        grace flows from your lips:
    therefore has God blessed you for ever and ever.

3. Gird your sword upon your thigh, O mighty warrior:
    in glory and majesty tread down your foes, and triumph!

4. Ride on in the cause of truth:
    and for the sake of justice.

5. Your right hand shall teach a terrible instruction:
    peoples shall fall beneath you, your arrows shall be sharp
    in the hearts of the king's enemies.

6. Your throne is the throne of God, it endures for ever:
    and the sceptre of your kingdom is a righteous sceptre.

7. You have loved righteousness and hated evil:
    therefore God, your God, has anointed you
   with the oil of gladness above your fellows.

8. All your garments are fragrant
    with myrrh, aloes and cassia:
   music from ivory palaces makes you glad.

9. Kings' daughters are among your noble women:
    the queen is at your right hand in gold of Ophir.

10. Hear, O daughter, consider and incline your ear:
    forget your own people and your father's house.

11. The king desires your beauty:
    he is your lord, therefore bow down before him.

12. The richest among the people, O daughter of Tyre:
    shall entreat your favour with gifts.

13. The king's daughter is all glorious within:
    her clothing is embroidered cloth-of-gold.

14. In robes of many colours she is led to you, O king:
    and, after her, the virgins that are with her.

15. They are led with gladness and rejoicing:
    they enter the palace of the king.

16. In place of your fathers you shall have sons:
    and make them princes over all the land.

17. And I will make known your name to every generation:
    therefore the peoples shall give you praise for ever.

Psalm 46

1. God is our refuge and strength:
    a very present help in trouble.

2. Therefore we will not fear, though the earth be moved:
    and though the mountains are shaken
   in the midst of the sea;

3. Though the waters rage and foam:
    and though the mountains quake at the rising of the sea.

4. There is a river whose streams make glad the city of God:
    the holy dwelling-place of the Most High.

5. God is in the midst of her,
        therefore she shall not be moved:
    God will help her, and at break of day.

6. The nations make uproar, and the kingdoms are shaken:
    but God has lifted his voice, and the earth shall tremble.

7. *The Lord of hosts is with us:*
    the God of Jacob is our stronghold.

7. Come then and see what the Lord has done:
    what destruction he has brought upon the earth.

8. He makes wars to cease in all the world:
        he breaks the bow and shatters the spear,
    and burns the chariots in the fire.

9. 'Be still, and know that I am God:
        I will be exalted among the nations,
    I will be exalted upon the earth.'

10. *The Lord of hosts is with us:*
    the God of Jacob is our stronghold.

Psalm 47

1. O clap your hands, all you peoples:
    and cry aloud to God with shouts of joy.

2. For the Lord Most High is to be feared:
    he is a great King over all the earth.

3. He cast down peoples under us:
    and the nations beneath our feet.

4. He chose us a land for our possession:
    that was the pride of Jacob, whom he loved.

5. God has gone up with the sound of rejoicing:
          and the Lord to the blast of the horn.

   6. O sing praises, sing praises to God:
          O sing praises, sing praises to our King.

   7. For God is the King of all the earth:
          O praise him in a well-wrought psalm.

   8. God has become the King of the nations:
          he has taken his seat upon his holy throne.

   9. The princes of the peoples are gathered together:
          with the people of the God of Abraham.

   10. For the mighty ones of the earth
          are become the servants of God:
       and he is greatly exalted.

Psalm 48

   1. Great is the Lord and greatly to be praised:
          in the city of our God.

   2. High and beautiful is his holy hill:
          it is the joy of all the earth.

   3. On Mount Zion, where godhead truly dwells,
          stands the city of the Great King:
       God is well known in her palaces as a sure defence.

   4. For the kings of the earth assembled:
          they gathered together and came on;

   5. They saw, they were struck dumb:
          they were astonished and fled in terror.

   6. Trembling took hold on them, and anguish:
          as on a woman in her travail;

   7. Like the breath of the east wind:
          that shatters the ships of Tarshish.

   8. As we have heard, so have we seen
          in the city of the Lord of hosts:

in the city of our God,
      which God has established for ever.

9. We have called to mind your loving-kindness, O God:
      in the midst of your temple.

10. As your name is great, O God, so also is your praise:
      even to the ends of the earth.

11. Your right hand is full of victory
         —let Zion's hill rejoice:
    let the daughters of Judah be glad,
         because of your judgements.

12. Walk about Zion, go round about her,
         and count all her towers:
    consider well her ramparts, pass through her palaces;

13. That you may tell those who come after that such is God:
      our God for ever and ever, and he will guide us eternally.

Psalm 49

1. O hear this, all you peoples:
      give ear, all you inhabitants of the world,

2. All children of men and sons of Adam:
      both rich and poor alike.

3. For my mouth shall speak wisdom:
      and the thoughts of my heart
   shall be full of understanding.

4. I will incline my ear to a riddle:
      and unfold the mystery to the sounds of the harp.

5. Why should I fear in the evil days:
      when the wickedness of my deceivers surrounds me,

6. Though they trust to their great wealth:
      and boast of the abundance of their riches?

7. No man may ransom his brother:
      or give God a price for him,

8. So that he may live for ever:
      and never see the grave;

9. For to ransom men's lives is so costly:
      that he must abandon it for ever.

10. For we see that wise men die:
      and perish with the foolish and the ignorant,
    leaving their wealth to others.

11. The tomb is their home for ever,
      their dwelling-place throughout all generations:
    though they called estates after their own names.

12. A rich man without understanding:
      is like the beasts that perish.

13. This is the lot of the foolish:
      the end of those who are pleased with their own words.

14. They are driven like sheep into the grave,
      and death is their shepherd:
    they slip down easily into the tomb

15. Their bright forms shall wear away in the grave:
      and lose their former glory.

16. But God will ransom my life:
      he will take me from the power of the grave.

17. Do not fear when a man grows rich:
      when the wealth of his household increases,

18. For he will take nothing away when he dies:
      nor will his wealth go down after him.

19. Though he counts himself happy while he lives:
      and praises you also when you prosper,

20. He will go to the company of his fathers:
      who will never see the light.

21. A rich man without understanding:
      is like the beasts that perish.

Psalm 50

1. The Lord our God, the Mighty One, has spoken:
    and summoned the earth,
   from the rising of the sun to its setting in the west.

2. From Zion, perfect in beauty:
    God has shone out in glory.

3. Our God is coming, he will not keep silent:
    before him is devouring fire,
   and tempest whirls about him.

4. He calls to the heavens above:
    and to the earth, so he may judge his people.

5. 'Gather to me my faithful ones:
    those who by sacrifice made a covenant with me.'

6. The heavens shall proclaim his righteousness:
    for God himself is judge.

7. 'Listen my people, and I will speak:
    O Israel, I am God your God,
   and I will give my testimony.

8. 'It is not for your sacrificees that I reprove you:
    For your burnt-offerings are always before me.

9. 'I will take no bull from your farms:
    or he-goat from your pens.

10. 'For all the beasts of the forest belong to me:
    and so do the cattle upon the mountains.

11. 'I know all the birds of the air:
    and the grasshoppers of the field are in my sight.

12. 'If I were hungry, I would not tell you:
    for the whole world is mine, and all that is in it.

13. 'Do I eat the flesh of bulls:
    or drink the blood of goats?

14. 'Offer to God a sacrifice of thanksgiving:
    and pay your vows to the Most High.

15. 'Call upon me in the day of trouble:
       I will bring you out, and you shall glorify me.'

16. But God says to the wicked:
       'What have you to do with reciting my laws,
    or taking my covenant on your lips,

17. 'Seeing you loathe discipline:
       and have tossed my words behind you?

18. 'When you saw a thief, you went along with him:
       and you threw in your lot with adulterers.

19. 'You have loosed your mouth in evil:
       and your tongue strings lies together.

20. 'You sit and speak against your brother:
       and slander your own mother's son.

21. 'These things you have done, and I held my tongue:
       and you thought I was just such another as yourself.

22. 'But I will convict you:
       and set before your eyes what you have done.

23. 'O consider this, you who forget God:
       lest I tear you in pieces, and there be no one to save you.

24. 'He honours me who brings sacrifice of thanksgiving:
       and to him who keeps to my way
    I will show the salvation of God.'

Psalm 51

1. Have mercy on me, O God, in your enduring goodness:
       according to the fulness of your compassion
    blot out my offences.

2. Wash me thoroughly from my wickedness:
       and cleanse me from my sin.

3. For I acknowledge my rebellion:
       and my sin is ever before me.

4. Against you only have I sinned
    and done what is evil in your eyes:

      so you will be just in your sentence
        and blameless in your judging.

5. Surely in wickedness I was brought to birth:
    and in sin my mother conceived me.

6. You that desire truth in the inward parts:
    O teach me wisdom in the secret places of the heart.

7. Purge me with hyssop, and I shall be clean:
    wash me, and I shall be whiter than snow.

8. Make me hear of joy and gladness:
    let the bones which you have broken rejoice.

9. Hide your face from my sins:
    and blot out all my iniquities.

10. Create in me a clean heart, O God:
    and renew a right spirit within me.

11. Do not cast me out from your presence:
    do not take your holy spirit from me.

12. O give me the gladness of your help again:
    and support me with a willing spirit.

13. Then will I teach transgressors your ways:
    and sinners shall turn to you again.

14. O Lord God of my salvation, deliver me from bloodshed:
    and my tongue shall sing of your righteousness.

15. O Lord, open my lips:
    and my mouth shall proclaim your praise.

16. You take no pleasure in sacrifice, or I would give it:
    burnt-offerings you do not want.

17. The sacrifice of God is a broken spirit:
    a broken and contrite heart, O God, you will not despise.

18. In your graciousness do good to Zion:
    rebuild the walls of Jerusalem.

19. Then will you delight in right sacrifices,
      in burnt-offerings and oblations:
  then will they offer young bulls upon your altar.

Psalm 52

1. Why, O man of power, do you boast all the day long:
    of mischief done to him that is faithful to God?

2. You contrive destroying slanders:
    your tongue is like a sharpened razor,
  it cuts deceitfully.

3. You have loved evil, and not good:
    to tell lies, rather than to speak the truth.

4. You love all words that may do hurt:
    and every deceit of the tongue.

5. But God will destroy you utterly:
    he will snatch you away
  and pluck you out of your dwelling,
    he will uproot you from the land of the living.

6. The righteous shall see it, and fear:
    they shall laugh you to scorn, and say,

7. 'Behold, this is the man
    who did not take God for his strength:
  but trusted in the abundance of his riches,
    and found his strength in slander.'

8. As for me, I am like a green olive tree in the house of God:
    I will trust in the goodness of God for ever and ever.

9. I will always give you thanks, for this was your doing:
    I will glorify your name before the faithful,
  for it is good to praise you.

Psalm 53

1. The fool has said in his heart 'There is no God':
    they have all become vile and abominable
  in their wickedness, there is not one that does good.

2. God looked down from heaven upon the children of men:
    to see if there were any who would act wisely
  and seek after God.

3. But they have all turned aside,
    they have all alike become corrupt:
  there is none that does good, no not one.

4. Are all the evildoers devoid of understanding:
    who eat up my people as men eat bread,
  and do not pray to God?

5. They shall be struck with terror:
    for God will scatter the bones of the ungodly.

6. They shall be put to confusion:
    because God has rejected them.

7. O that deliverance for Israel might come forth from Zion:
    when the Lord turns again the fortunes of his people,
  then shall Jacob rejoice and Israel be glad.

Psalm 54

1. Save me, O God, by the power of your name:
    and vindicate me by your might.

2. Hear my prayer, O God:
    and listen to the words of my mouth.

3. For the insolent have risen against me:
    ruthless men, who have not set God before them,
  seek my life.

4. But surely God is my helper:
    the Lord is the upholder of my life.

5. [Let evil recoil on those that would waylay me:
    O destroy them in your faithfulness!]

6. Then will I offer you sacrifice with a willing heart:
    I will praise your name, O Lord, for it is good.

7. For you will deliver me from every trouble:
    my eyes shall see the downfall of my enemies.

Psalm 55

1. Hear my prayer, O God:
    and do not hide yourself from my petition.
2. Give heed to me, and answer me:
    I am restless in my complaining.
3. I am in turmoil at the voice of the enemy:
    at the onslaught of the wicked.
4. For they bring down disaster upon me:
    they persecute me with bitter fury.
5. My heart writhes within me:
    and the terrors of death have fallen upon me.
6. Fear and trembling come upon me:
    and horror overwhelms me.
7. And I said 'O for the wings of a dove:
    that I might fly away and find rest.
8. 'Then I would flee far off:
    and make my lodging in the wilderness.
9. 'I would hasten to find me a refuge:
    out of the blast of slander,
10. 'Out of the tempest of their calumny, O Lord:
    and far from their double tongues.'
11. For I have seen violence and strife in the city:
    day and night they go round it upon its walls.
12. Evil and wickedness are within it:
    iniquity is within it, oppression and fraud
    do not depart from its streets.
13. It was not an enemy that reviled me,
    or I might have borne it:
    it was not my foe that dealt so insolently with me,
    or I might have hidden myself from him;
14. But it was you, a man like myself:
    my companion and my familiar friend.

15. Together we enjoyed sweet fellowship:
    in the house of our God.

16. [Let them pass away in confusion:
    let death carry them to destruction;

17. Let them go down alive to Sheol:
    for evil is among them in their dwellings.]

18. But I will call to God:
    and the Lord my God will save me.

19. At evening, at morning, and at noon-day:
    I complain and groan aloud.

20. And he will hear my voice:
    and ransom my soul in peace,

21. From those that bear down upon me:
    for there are many against me.

22. God will hear and bring them low:
    he that is enthroned for ever.

23. For they do not keep their word:
    and they have no fear of God.

24. They lay violent hands
      on those that are at peace with them:
    they break solemn covenants.

25. Their mouths are smooth as butter,
      but war is in their hearts:
    their words are softer than oil,
      yet they are drawn swords.

26. Cast your burden on the Lord, and he will sustain you:
    he will never suffer the righteous man to stumble.

27. But as for them, you will bring them down, O God:
    even to the depths of the Pit.

28. Bloodthirsty and deceitful men
      shall not live out half their days:
    but I will trust in you.

Psalm 56

1. Be merciful to me, O God, for men are treading me down:
    all day long my adversary presses upon me.
2. My enemies tread me down all the day:
    for there are many that arrogantly fight against me.
3. In the hour of fear:
    I will put my trust in you.
4. In God, whose word I praise, in God I trust and fear not:
    what can flesh do to me?
5. All day long they afflict me with their words:
    and every thought is how to do me evil.
6. They stir up hatred and conceal themselves:
    they watch my steps, while they lie in wait for my life.
7. Let there be no escape for them:
    bring down the peoples in your wrath, O God.
8. You have counted my anxious tossings;
        put my tears in your bottle:
    are not these things noted in your book?
9. In the day that I call to you, my enemies shall turn back:
    this I know, for God is with me.
10. In God, whose word I praise, in God I trust and fear not:
    what can man do to me?
11. To you, O God, must I perform my vows:
    I will pay the thank-offering that is due.
12. For you will deliver my soul from death,
        and my feet from falling:
    that I may walk before God in the light of the living.

Psalm 57

1. Be merciful to me, O God, be merciful:
    for I come to you for shelter;

2. And in the shadow of your wings will I take refuge:
    until these troubles are over-past.

3. I will call to God Most High:
    to the God who will fulfil his purpose for me.

4. He will send from heaven and save me:
    he will send forth his faithfulness and his loving-kindness,
  and rebuke those that would trample me down.

5. For I lie amidst ravening lions:
    men whose teeth are spears and arrows,
  and their tongue a sharpened sword.

6. *Be exalted, O God, above the heavens:*
    and let your glory be over all the earth.

7. They have set a net for my feet, and I am brought low:
    they have dug a pit before me,
  but shall fall into it themselves.

8. My heart is fixed, O God, my heart is fixed:
    I will sing and make melody.

9. Awake my soul, awake lute and harp:
    for I will awaken the morning.

10. I will give you thanks, O Lord, among the peoples:
    I will sing your praise among the nations.

11. For the greatness of your mercy reaches to the heavens:
    and your faithfulness to the clouds.

12. *Be exalted, O God, above the heavens:*
    and let your glory be over all the earth.

Psalm 58

1. [Do you indeed decree what is just, O rulers:
    do you with uprightness judge the children of men?

2. No, you work in the land with evil heart:
    you look on the violence that your hands have wrought.

3. The wicked are estranged, even from the womb:
   they are liars that go astray from their birth.

4. They are venomous with the venom of serpents:
   like the deaf asp that stops its ears,

5. And will not heed the voice of the charmers:
   though the binder of spells be skilful.

6. Break their teeth, O God, in their mouths:
   shatter the jaws of the young lions, O Lord.

7. Let them dissolve, and drain away like water:
   let them be trodden down, let them wither like grass,

8. Like a woman's miscarriage that melts and passes away:
   like an abortive birth that has not seen the sun.

9. Before they know it, let them be cut down like thorns:
   like brambles which a man sweeps angrily aside.

10. The righteous shall rejoice when he sees the vengeance:
    he will wash his feet in the blood of the ungodly.

11. And men will say 'There is reward for the righteous:
    there is indeed a God who judges on earth.']

Psalm 59

1. Deliver me from my enemies, O God:
   lift me to safety from those that rise against me;

2. O deliver me from the evildoers:
   and save me from bloodthirsty men.

3. For they lie in wait for my life:
   savage men stir up violence against me.

4. Not for my sin or my transgression, O Lord,
       not for any evil I have done:
   do they run and take up position against me.

5. Arise to meet me, and see:
   you that are Lord of hosts and God of Israel.

6. [Awake to punish all the nations:
    have no mercy on those that so treacherously do wrong.]

7. They return every evening, they howl like dogs:
    they prowl around the city.

8. Look how their mouths slaver:
    swords strike from their lips,
   for they say 'Who will hear it?'

9. But you, O Lord, will laugh them to scorn:
    you will deride all the nations.

10. I will look to you, O my strength:
    for God is my strong tower.

11. My God in his steadfastness will come to meet me:
    God will show me the downfall of my enemies.

12. Slay them not, O Lord, lest my people forget:
    but make them stagger by your power,
    and bring them down.

13. Give them over to punishment for the sin of their mouths,
        for the words of their lips:
    let them be taken in their pride.

14. [For the curses and lies that they have uttered,
        O consume them in your wrath:
    Consume them, till they are no more;]

15. That men may know that God rules over Jacob:
    even to the ends of the earth.

16. They return every evening, they howl like dogs:
    they prowl around the city.

17. They roam here and there looking for food:
    and growl if they are not filled.

18. But I will sing of your might:
    I will sing aloud each morning of your goodness.

19. For you have been my strong tower:
    and a sure refuge in the day of my distress.

20. I will sing your praises, O my strength:
    for God is my strong tower.

Psalm 60

1. O God, you have cast us off and broken us:
    you were enraged against us—O restore us again!
2. You have caused the land to quake, you have rent it open:
    heal the rifts, for the earth quivers and breaks.
3. You have steeped your people in a bitter draught:
    you have given them a wine to make them stagger.
4. You have caused those that fear you to take flight:
    so that they run from the bow.
5. O save us by your right hand, and answer us:
    that those whom you love may be delivered.
6. God has said in his holy place:
    'I will exult and divide Shechem,
    I will parcel out the valley of Succoth.
7. 'Gilead is mine, and Manasseh is mine:
    Ephraim is my helmet, and Judah my rod of command.
8. 'Moab is my wash-bowl, over Edom will I cast my shoe:
    against Philistia will I shout in triumph.'
9. Who will lead me into the fortified city:
    who will bring me into Edom?
10. Have you not cast us off, O God?:
    you go not out with our armies.
11. Give us your help against the enemy:
    for vain is the help of man.
12. By the power of our God we shall do valiantly:
    for it is he that will tread down our enemies.

Psalm 61

1. Hear my loud crying, O God:
    and give heed to my prayer.
2. From the ends of the earth I call to you
    when my heart faints:
    O set me on the rock that is higher than I.

3. For you have been my refuge:
    and my strong tower against the enemy.

4. I will dwell in your tent for ever:
    and find shelter in the covering of your wings.

5. For you have heard my vows, O God:
    you have granted the desire of those that fear your name.

6. You will give the king long life:
    and his years shall endure through many generations.

7. He shall dwell before God for ever:
    loving-kindness and truth shall be his guard.

8. So will I ever sing praises to your name:
    while I daily perform my vows.

Psalm 62

1. My soul waits in silence for God:
    for from him comes my salvation.

2. He only is my rock and my salvation:
    my strong tower, so that I shall never be moved.

3. How long will you all plot against a man to destroy him:
    as though he were a leaning fence or a buckling wall?

4. Their design is to thrust him from his height,
      and their delight is in lies:
    they bless with their lips, but inwardly they curse.

5. Nevertheless, my soul, wait in silence for God:
    for from him comes my hope.

6. He only is my rock and my salvation:
    my strong tower, so that I shall not be moved.

7. In God is my deliverance and my glory:
    God is my strong rock and my shelter.

8. Trust in him at all times, O my people:
    pour out your hearts before him, for God is our refuge.

9. The children of men are but breath,
    the children of men are a lie:
   place them in the scales and they fly upward,
    they are as light as air.

10. Put no trust in extortion,
     do not grow worthless by robbery:
    if riches increase, set not your heart upon them.

11. God has spoken once, twice have I heard him say:
     that power belongs to God,

12. That to the Lord belongs a constant goodness:
     for you reward a man according to his works.

Psalm 63

1. O God, you are my God:
    eagerly will I seek you.

2. My soul thirsts for you, my flesh longs for you:
    as a dry and thirsty land where no water is.

3. So it was when I beheld you in the sanctuary:
    and saw your power and your glory.

4. For your unchanging goodness is better than life:
    therefore my lips shall praise you.

5. And so I will bless you as long as I live:
    and in your name will I lift my hands on high.

6. My longing shall be satisfied as with marrow and fatness:
    my mouth shall praise you with exultant lips.

7. When I remember you upon my bed:
    when I meditate upon you in the night watches,

8. How you have been my helper:
    then I sing for joy in the shadow of your wings,

9. Then my soul clings to you:
    and your right hand upholds me.

10. Those that seek my life are marked for destruction:
   they shall go down to the deep places of the earth.

11. They shall be delivered to the sword:
   they shall be a portion for jackals.

12. The king will rejoice in God,
   and all who take oaths on his name shall glory:
  but the mouths of liars shall be stopped.

Psalm 64

1. Hear my voice, O God, in my complaining:
   preserve my life from fear of the enemy.

2. Hide me from the conspiracy of the wicked:
   from the throng of evildoers,

3. Who sharpen their tongues like swords:
   who string the bow, who take arrows of bitter words,

4. To shoot from hiding at the blameless man:
   to strike at him suddenly and unseen.

5. They are confirmed in an evil purpose:
   they confide it to one another while they lay the snares,
  saying 'Who will see them?'

6. They hatch mischief, they hide a well-considered plan:
   for the mind and heart of man is very deep.

7. But God will shoot at them with his swift arrows:
   they shall be suddenly struck through.

8. The Lord will bring them down
   for what their tongues have spoken:
  and all that see it shall toss their heads in scorn.

9. Then all men shall fear:
   and tell what the Lord has done, and ponder his works.

10. The righteous man shall rejoice in the Lord,
   and find in him his refuge:
  and all the upright in heart shall exult.

Psalm 65

1. You are to be praised, O God, in Zion:
    to you shall vows be paid, you that answer prayer.

2. To you shall all flesh come to confess their sins:
    when our misdeeds prevail against us,
  you will purge them away.

3. Blessed is the man whom you choose and take to yourself
    to dwell within your courts:
  we shall be filled with the good things of your house,
    of your holy temple.

4. You will answer us in your righteousness
    with terrible deeds, O God our saviour:
  you that are the hope of all the ends of the earth
    and of the distant seas;

5. Who by your strength made fast the mountains:
    you that are girded with power;

6. Who stilled the raging of the seas,
    the roaring of the waves:
  and the tumult of the peoples.

7. Those who dwell at the ends of the earth
    are afraid at your wonders:
  the dawn and the evening sing your praises.

8. You tend the earth and water it:
    you make it rich and fertile.

9. The river of God is full of water:
    and so providing for the earth,
  you provide grain for men.

10. You drench its furrows, you level the ridges between:
    you soften it with showers and bless its early growth.

11. You crown the year with your goodness:
    and the tracks where you have passed drip with fatness.

12. The pastures of the wilderness run over:
    and the hills are girded with joy.

13. The meadows are clothed with sheep:
    and the valleys stand so thick with corn,
    they shout for joy and sing.

Psalm 66

1. O shout with joy to God, all the earth:
    sing to the honour of his name,
    and give him glory as his praise.

2. Say to God 'How fearful are your works:
    because of your great might
    your enemies shall cower before you'.

3. All the earth shall worship you:
    and sing to you, and sing praises to your name.

4. Come then and see what God has done:
    how terrible are his dealings with the children of men.

5. He turned the sea into dry land,
    they crossed the river on foot:
    then were we joyful because of him.

6. By his power he rules for ever,
    his eyes keep watch on the nations:
    and rebels shall never rise against him.

7. O bless our God, you peoples:
    and cause his praises to resound,

8. Who has held our souls in life:
    who has not suffered our feet to slip.

9. For you have proved us, O God:
    you have tried us as silver is tried.

10. You brought us into the net:
    you laid sharp torment on our loins.

11. You let men ride over our heads,
    we went through fire and water:
    but you brought us out into a place of liberty.

12. I will come into your house with burnt-offerings:
    and I will pay you my vows,

13. The vows that opened my lips:
    that my mouth uttered when I was in trouble.

14. I will offer you burnt-offerings of fattened beasts,
    with the sweet smoke of rams:
    I will sacrifice a bull and the flesh of goats.

15. Come then and hear, all you that fear God:
    and I will tell what he has done for me.

16. I called to him with my mouth:
    and his praise was on my tongue.

17. If I had cherished wickedness in my heart:
    the Lord would not have heard me.

18. But God has heard me:
    he has heeded the voice of my prayer.

19. Praise be to God:
    who has not turned back my prayer,
    or his steadfast love from me.

Psalm 67

1. Let God be gracious to us and bless us:
   and make his face shine upon us,

2. That your ways may be known on earth:
   your liberating power among all nations.

3. Let the peoples praise you, O God:
   let all the peoples praise you.

4. Let the nations be glad and sing:
   for you judge the peoples with integrity,
   and govern the nations upon earth.

5. Let the peoples praise you, O God:
   let all the peoples praise you.

6. Then the earth will yield its fruitfulness:
   and God, our God, will bless us.

7. God shall bless us:
   and all the ends of the earth will fear him.

Psalm 68

1. God shall arise, and his enemies shall be scattered:
    those that hate him shall flee before his face.

2. As smoke is dispersed, so shall they be dispersed:
    as wax melts before a fire,
   so shall the wicked perish at the presence of God.

3. But the righteous shall be glad and exult before God:
    they shall rejoice with gladness.

4. O sing to God, sing praises to his name:
    glorify him that rode through the deserts,
   him whose name is the Lord, and exult before him.

5. He is the father of the fatherless,
    he upholds the cause of the widow:
   God in his holy dwelling place.

6. He gives the desolate a home to dwell in,
    and brings the prisoners out into prosperity:
   but rebels must dwell in a barren land.

7. O God, when you went out before your people:
    when you marched through the wilderness,

8. The earth shook, the heavens poured down water:
    before the God of Sinai, before God, the God of Israel.

9. You showered down a generous rain, O God:
    you prepared the land of your possession
   when it was weary.

10. And there your people settled:
     in the place that your goodness, O God,
    had made ready for the poor.

11. The Lord spoke the word, and great was the company
     of those that carried the tidings:
    'Kings with their armies are fleeing, are fleeing away.

12. 'Even the women at home may share in the spoil:
     and will you sit idly among the sheepfolds?

13. 'There are images of doves whose wings are covered with silver:
    and their pinions with shining gold.'

14. When the Almighty scattered kings:
    they were like snow falling upon Mount Zalmon.

15. The mountain of Bashan is a mighty mountain:
    the mountain of Bashan is a mountain of many peaks.

16. O mountains of many peaks, why look so enviously:
    at the mountain where God is pleased to dwell,
    where the Lord will remain for ever?

17. The chariots of God are twice ten thousand,
        and thousands upon thousands:
    the Lord came from Sinai into his holy place.

18. When you ascended the heights,
        you led the enemy captive,
    you received tribute from men:
        but rebels shall not dwell in the presence of God.

19. Blessed be the Lord day by day,
        who bears us as his burden:
    he is the God of our deliverance.

20. God is to us a God who saves:
    by God the Lord do we escape death.

21. [But God shall smite the heads of his enemies:
    the hairy scalp of those that walk in their sins.

22. The Lord said 'I will bring them back from Bashan:
    I will bring them again from the deep sea';

23. That you may dip your feet in blood:
        and the tongues of your dogs
    in the blood of your enemies.]

24. Your procession is seen, O God:
    the procession of my God and King in the sanctuary.

25. The singers go before, the musicians come after:
    and around them the maidens beating on the timbrels.

26. In their choirs they bless God:
    those that are sprung from the fount of Israel
   bless the Lord.

27. There is the little tribe of Benjamin leading them:
    the throng of the princes of Judah,
   the princes of Zebulun and the princes of Naphtali.

28. Give the command, my God,
    in accordance with your power:
   that godlike power whereby you act for us.

29. Give the command from your temple at Jerusalem:
    and kings shall bring you tribute.

30. Rebuke the beast of the reeds,
    the herd of bulls amidst the brutish peoples:
   tread down those that are greedy for silver,
    scatter the peoples that relish war.

31. Let them bring bronze from Egypt:
    let the hands of the Nubians carry it swiftly to God.

32. Sing to God, you kingdoms of the earth:
    O sing praises to the Lord,

33. To him that rides upon the highest heavens,
    that were from the beginning:
   who utters his voice, which is a mighty voice.

34. Ascribe power to God, whose majesty is over Israel:
    and his might is in the clouds.

35. Terrible is God who comes from his holy place:
    the God of Israel who gives
   power and strength to his people. Blessed be God.

Psalm 69

1. Save me, O God:
    for the waters have come up even to my throat.

2. I sink in the deep mire where no footing is:
    I have come into deep waters
   and the flood sweeps over me.

3. I am weary with crying out, my throat is parched:
    my eyes fail with watching so long for my God.

4. Those that hate me without cause
      are more in number than the hairs of my head:
    those that would destroy me are many,
      they oppose me wrongfully
    —for I must restore things that I never took.

5. O God, you know my foolishness:
    and my sins are not hidden from you.

6. Let not those who wait for you be shamed because of me,
      O Lord God of hosts:
    let not those who seek you be disgraced on my account,
      O God of Israel.

7. For your sake have I suffered reproach:
    and shame has covered my face.

8. I have become a stranger to my brothers:
    an alien to my own mother's sons.

9. Zeal for your house has eaten me up:
    and the taunts of those who taunt you have fallen on me.

10. I afflicted myself with fasting:
     and that was turned to my reproach.

11. I made sackcloth my clothing:
     and I became a byword to them.

12. Those who sit in the gate talk of me:
     and the drunkards make songs about me.

13. But to you, Lord, I make my prayer:
     at an acceptable time.

14. Answer me, O God, in your abundant goodness:
     and with your sure deliverance.

15. Bring me out of the mire, so that I may not sink:
     let me be delivered from my enemies,
    and from the deep waters.

16. Let not the flood overwhelm me
    or the depths swallow me up:
  let not the Pit shut its mouth upon me.

17. Hear me, O Lord, as your loving-kindness is good:
    turn to me, as your compassion is great.

18. Do not hide your face from your servant:
    for I am in trouble—O be swift to answer me!

19. Draw near to me and redeem me:
    O ransom me because of my enemies!

20. You know all their taunts:
    my adversaries are all in your sight.

21. Insults have broken my heart:
    my shame and disgrace are past healing.

22. I looked for someone to have pity on me,
      but there was no man:
    for some to comfort me, but found none.

23. They gave me poison for food:
    and when I was thirsty, they gave me vinegar to drink.

24. [Let their table become a snare:
    and their sacrificial feasts a trap.

25. Let their eyes be darkened, so that they cannot see:
    and make their loins shake continually.

26. Pour out your wrath upon them:
    and let your fierce anger overtake them.

27. Let their camp be desolate:
    and let no man dwell in their tents.

28. For they persecute him whom you have stricken:
    and multiply the pain of him whom you have wounded.

29. Let them have punishment upon punishment:
    let them not receive your forgiveness.

30. Let them be blotted out of the book of the living:
    let them not be written down among the righteous.]

The Psalms

31. As for me, I am poor and in misery:
    O God, let your deliverance lift me up.

32. And I will praise the name of God in a song:
    and glorify him with thanksgiving.

33. And that will please the Lord more than an ox:
    more than a bull with horns and cloven hoof.

34. Consider this, you that are meek, and rejoice:
    seek God, and let your heart be glad.

35. For the Lord listens to the poor:
    he does not despise his servants in captivity.

36. Let the heavens and the earth praise him:
    the seas and all that moves in them.

37. For God will save Zion:
    he will rebuild the cities of Judah.

38. His people shall live there and possess it,
    the seed of his servants shall inherit it:
    and those who love his name shall dwell in it.

Psalm 70

1. O God, be pleased to deliver me:
   O Lord, make haste to help me.

2. Let them be put to shame and confounded
   who seek my life:
   let them be turned back and disgraced who wish me evil.

3. Let them turn away for shame:
   who say to me 'Aha, aha!'

4. Let all who seek you be joyful and glad because of you:
   let those who love your salvation say always 'God is great.'

5. As for me, I am poor and needy:
   O God, be swift to save me.

6. You are my helper and my deliverer:
   O Lord, make no delay.

Psalm 71

1. To you, Lord, have I come for shelter:
    let me never be put to shame.

2. In your righteousness rescue and deliver me:
    incline your ear to me and save me.

3. Be for me a rock of refuge, a fortress to defend me:
    for you are my high rock, and my stronghold.

4. Rescue me, O my God, from the hand of the wicked:
    from the grasp of the pitiless and unjust.

5. For you, Lord, are my hope:
    you are my confidence, O God, from my youth upward.

6. On you have I leaned since my birth:
    you are he that brought me out of my mother's womb,
  and my praise is of you continually.

7. I have become as a fearful warning to many:
    but you are my strength and my refuge.

8. My mouth shall be filled with your praises:
    I shall sing of your glory all the day long.

9. Cast me not away in the time of old age:
    nor forsake me when my strength fails.

10. For my enemies speak against me:
    and those that watch for my life
  conspire together, saying,

11. 'God has forsaken him:
    pursue him, take him, for there is none to save him.'

12. Be not far from me, O God:
    my God, make haste to help me.

13. Let my adversaries be confounded and put to shame:
    let those who seek my hurt
  be covered with scorn and disgrace.

14. As for me, I will wait in hope continually:
    and I will praise you more and more.

15. My mouth shall speak of your righteousness all the day:
        and tell of your salvation, though it exceeds my telling.

16. I will begin with the mighty acts of the Lord my God:
        and declare your righteous dealing—yours alone.

17. O God, you have taught me from my youth upward:
        and to this day, I proclaim your marvellous works.

18. Forsake me not, O God, in my old age,
        when I am grey-headed:
    till I have shown the strength of your arm
        to future generations, and your might
    to those that come after.

19. Your righteousness, O God, reaches to the heavens:
        great are the things that you have done;
    O God, who is like you?

20. You have burdened me with many and bitter troubles,
        O turn and renew me:
    and raise me up again from the depths of the earth.

21. Bless me beyond my former greatness:
        O turn to me again, and comfort me.

22. Then will I praise you upon the lute
        for your faithfulness, O my God:
    and sing your praises to the harp, O Holy One of Israel.

23. My lips shall rejoice in my singing:
        and my soul also, for you have ransomed me.

24. My tongue shall speak of your righteous dealing
        all the day long:
    for they shall be put to shame and disgraced
        that seek to do me evil.

Psalm 72

1. Give the king your judgement, O God:
        and your righteousness to the son of a king,

2. That he may judge your people rightly:
        and the poor of the land with equity.

3. Let the mountains be laden with peace
     because of his righteousness:
   and the hills also with prosperity for his people.

4. May he give justice to the poor among the people:
     and rescue the children of the needy,
   and crush the oppressor.

5. May he live while the sun endures:
     and while the moon gives light, throughout all generations.

6. May he come down like rain upon the new-mown fields:
     and as showers that water the earth.

7. In his time shall righteousness flourish:
     and abundance of peace, till the moon shall be no more.

8. His dominion shall stretch from sea to sea:
     from the Great River to the ends of the earth.

9. His adversaries shall bow down before him:
     and his enemies shall lick the dust.

10. The kings of Tarshish and of the isles
      shall bring tribute:
    the kings of Sheba and Seba shall offer gifts.

11. All kings shall fall down before him:
      and all nations do him service.

12. He will deliver the needy when they cry:
      and the poor man that has no helper.

13. He will pity the helpless and the needy:
      and save the lives of the poor.

14. He will redeem them from oppression and violence:
      and their blood shall be precious in his sight.

15. Long may he live, and be given of the gold of Sheba:
      may prayer be made for him continually,
    and men bless him every day.

16. Let there be abundance of wheat in the land:
      let it flourish on the tops of the mountains;

17. Let its ears grow fat like the grain of Lebanon:
      and its sheaves thicken like the grass of the field.

18. Let his name live for ever:
     and endure as long as the sun.
19. Let all peoples use his name in blessing:
     and all nations call him blessed.
20. Blessed be the Lord God, the God of Israel:
     who alone does great wonders.
21. Blessed be his glorious name for ever:
     and let the whole earth be filled with his glory.
    Amen, Amen.

Psalm 73

1. God is indeed good to Israel:
    to those whose hearts are pure.
2. Nevertheless, my feet were almost gone:
    my steps had well-nigh slipped.
3. For I was filled with envy at the boastful:
    when I saw the ungodly had such tranquillity.
4. For they suffer no pain:
    and their bodies are hale and fat.
5. They come to no misfortune like other folk:
    nor are they plagued like other men.
6. Therefore they put on pride as a necklace:
    And clothe themselves in violence as in a garment.
7. Their eyes shine from folds of fatness:
    and they have all that heart could wish.
8. Their talk is malice and mockery:
    and they hand down slanders from on high.
9. Their mouths blaspheme against heaven:
    and their tongues go to and fro on earth.
10. Therefore my people turn to them:
     and find in them no fault.
11. They say 'How can God know:
     is there understanding in the Most High?'

12. Behold, these are the ungodly:
     yet they prosper and increase in riches.

13. Was it for nothing then that I cleansed my heart:
     and washed my hands in innocence?

14. Have I been stricken all day long in vain:
     and rebuked every morning?

15. If I had said 'I will speak thus':
     I should have betrayed the family of your children.

16. Then I thought to understand this:
     but it was too hard for me,

17. Till I went into the sanctuary of God:
     and then I understood what their end will be.

18. For you set them in slippery places:
     and cause them to fall from their treacherous footholds.

19. How suddenly they are laid waste:
     they come to an end, they perish in terror.

20. As with a dream when one awakes:
     so when you rouse yourself, O Lord,
  you will despise their image.

21. When my heart was soured:
     and I was wounded to the core,

22. I was but brutish and ignorant:
     no better than a beast before you.

23. Nevertheless, I am always with you:
     for you hold me by my right hand.

24. You will guide me with your counsel:
     and afterwards you will lead me to glory.

25. Whom have I in heaven but you?:
     and there is no one upon earth
  that I desire in comparison with you.

26. Though my flesh and my heart fail me:
     you, O God, are my portion for ever.

27. Behold, those who forsake you shall perish:
    and all who whore after other gods you will destroy.

28. But it is good for me to draw near to God:
    I have made the Lord God my refuge,
    and I will tell of all that you have done.

Psalm 74

1. O Lord our God, why cast us off so utterly:
    why does your anger burn
    against the sheep of your pasture?

2. Remember your congregation,
     whom you took to yourself of old:
    the people that you redeemed to be your own possession,
     and Mount Zion where you have dwelt.

3. Rouse yourself and go to the utter ruins:
    to all the harm that the enemy has done in the sanctuary.

4. Your adversaries have made uproar
     in the place appointed for your praise:
    they have set up their standards in triumph.

5. They have destroyed on every side:
    like those who take axes up to a thicket of trees.

6. All the carved woodwork they have broken down:
    and smashed it with hammers and hatchets.

7. They have set fire to your sanctuary:
    and defiled to the ground the dwelling-place of your name.

8. They have said in their hearts
     'Let us make havoc of them':
    they have burned down
     all the holy places of God in the land.

9. We see no signs, there is not one prophet left:
    there is none who knows how long these things shall be.

10. How long shall the adversary taunt you, O God:
    shall the enemy blaspheme your name for ever?

11. Why do you hold back your hand:
    why do you keep your right hand in your bosom?

12. Yet God is my king from of old:
    who wrought deliverance upon the earth.

13. You divided the sea by your might:
    you shattered the heads of the dragons in the waters.

14. You crushed the heads of Leviathan:
    and gave him as food to the creatures of the desert waste.

15. You cleft open spring and fountain:
    you dried up the everflowing waters.

16. The day is yours, and so also is the night:
    you have established the moon and the sun.

17. You set all the boundaries of the earth:
    you created winter and summer.

18. Remember, O Lord, the taunts of the enemy:
    how a mindless people have blasphemed your name.

19. Do not give to the wild beasts the soul that praises you:
    do not forget for ever the life of your afflicted.

20. Look on all that you have made:
    for it is full of darkness,
    and violence inhabits the earth.

21. Let not the oppressed and reviled turn away rejected:
    but let the poor and needy praise your name.

22. Arise, O God, plead your own cause:
    remember how a mindless people taunt you all day long.

23. Do not forget the clamour of your adversaries:
    or how the shouting of your enemies ascends continually.

Psalm 75

1. We give you thanks, O God, we give you thanks:
   we call upon your name
   and tell of all the wonders you have done.

2. 'I will surely appoint a time:
    when I, the Lord, will judge with equity.

3. 'Though the earth shake, and all who dwell in it:
    it is I that have founded its pillars.

4. 'I will say to the boasters "Boast no more":
    and to the wicked "Do not flaunt your horns;

5. '"Do not flaunt your horns so high:
    or speak so proud and stiff-necked."'

6. For there is none from the east or from the west:
    or from the wilderness who can raise up;

7. But it is God who is the judge:
    who puts down one and exalts another.

8. For there is a cup in the Lord's hand:
    and the wine foams and is richly mixed;

9. He gives it in turn to each of the wicked of the earth:
    they drink it and drain it to the dregs.

10. But I will sing praises to the God of Jacob:
    I will glorify his name for ever.

11. All the horns of the wicked I will break:
    but the horns of the righteous shall be lifted high.

Psalm 76

1. In Judah God is known:
    his name is great in Israel.

2. At Salem is his tabernacle:
    and his dwelling is in Zion.

3. There he broke in pieces the flashing arrows of the bow:
    the shield, the sword and the weapons of battle.

4. Radiant in light are you:
    greater in majesty than the eternal hills.

5. The valiant were dumbfounded, they sleep their sleep:
    and all the men of war have lost their strength.

6. At the blast of your voice, O God of Jacob:
    both horse and chariot were cast asleep.

7. Terrible are you, Lord God:
    and who may stand before you when you are angry?

8. You caused your sentence to be heard from heaven:
    the earth feared and was still,

9. When God arose to judgement:
    to save all the meek of the earth.

10. For you crushed the wrath of man:
    you bridled the remnant of the wrathful.

11. O make vows to the Lord your God, and keep them:
    let all around him bring gifts
    to him that is worthy to be feared.

12. For he cuts down the fury of princes:
    and he is terrible to the kings of the earth.

Psalm 77

1. I call to my God, I cry out toward him:
    I call to my God, and surely he will answer.

2. In the day of my distress I seek the Lord,
    I stretch out my hands to him by night:
    my soul is poured out without ceasing,
    it refuses all comfort.

3. I think upon God and groan aloud:
    I muse, and my spirit faints.

4. You hold my eyelids open:
    I am so dazed that I cannot flee.

5. I consider the times that are past:
    I remember the years of long ago.

6. At night I am grieved to the heart:
    I ponder, and my spirit makes search;

7. 'Will the Lord cast us off for ever:
    will he show us his favour no more?

8. 'Is his mercy clean gone for ever:
       and his promise come to an end for all generations?

9. 'Has God forgotten to be gracious:
       has he shut up his pity in displeasure?'

10. And I say 'Has the right hand of the Most High
        lost its strength:
    has the arm of the Lord changed?'

11. I will declare the mighty acts of the Lord:
        I will call to mind your wonders of old.

12. I will think on all that you have done:
        and meditate upon your works.

13. Your way, O God, is holy:
        who is so great a god as our God?

14. You are the God that works wonders:
        you made known your power among the nations;

15. By your mighty arm you redeemed your people:
        the children of Jacob and Joseph.

16. The waters saw you, O God,
        the waters saw you and were afraid:
    the depths also were troubled.

17. The clouds poured out water, the heavens spoke:
        and your arrows darted forth.

18. The voice of your thunder was heard in the whirlwind:
        your lightnings lit the world,
    the earth shuddered and quaked.

19. Your way was in the sea, your path in the great waters:
        and your footsteps were not seen.

20. You led your people like sheep:
        by the hand of Moses and Aaron.

Psalm 78

1. Give heed to my teaching, O my people:
       incline your ears to the words of my mouth;

2. For I will open my mouth in a parable:
     and expound the mysteries of former times.

3. What we have heard and known:
     what our forefathers have told us,

4. We will not hide from their children,
     but declare to a generation yet to come:
   the praiseworthy acts of the Lord,
     his mighty and wonderful works.

5. He established a law in Jacob
     and made a decree in Israel:
   which he commanded our forefathers
     to teach their children.

6. That future generations might know,
     and the children yet unborn:
   that they in turn might teach it to their sons;

7. So that they might put their confidence in God:
     and not forget his works, but keep his commandments,

8. And not be as their forefathers,
     a stubborn and rebellious generation:
   a generation that did not set their heart aright,
     whose spirit was not faithful to God.

9. The children of Ephraim, armed with the bow:
     turned back in the day of battle.

10. They did not keep God's covenant,
      they refused to walk in his law:
    they forgot what he had done,
      and the wonders he had shown them.

11. For he did marvellous things in the sight of their fathers:
      in the land of Egypt, in the country of Zoan.

12. He divided the sea and let them pass through:
      he made the waters stand up in a heap.

13. In the daytime he led them with a cloud:
      and all night long with the light of fire.

14. He cleft rocks in the wilderness:
    and gave them drink in abundance
    as from springs of water.

15. He brought streams out of the rock:
    and caused the waters to flow down like rivers.

16. But for all this they sinned yet more against him:
    and rebelled against the Most High in the desert.

17. They wilfully put God to the test:
    and demanded food for their appetite.

18. They spoke against God, and said:
    'Can God prepare a table in the wilderness?

19. 'He indeed struck the rock,
    so that the waters gushed and the streams overflowed:
    but can he also give bread,
    or provide meat for his people?'

20. When the Lord heard it he was angry,
    and a fire was kindled against Jacob:
    his wrath blazed against Israel.

21. For they put no trust in God:
    nor would they believe his power to save.

22. Then he commanded the clouds above:
    and opened the doors of heaven.

23. He rained down manna for them to eat:
    and gave them the grain of heaven.

24. So men ate the bread of angels:
    and he sent them food in abundance.

25. He stirred up the south east wind in the heavens:
    and guided it by his power.

26. He rained down meat upon them thick as dust:
    and winged birds like the sands of the sea.

27. He made them fall into the midst of their camp:
    and all about their tents.

28. So they ate and were well-filled:
    for he had given them what they desired.

29. But before they had satisfied their craving:
    while the food was still in their mouths,

30. The anger of God blazed up against them:
    and he slew their strongest men,
    and laid low the youth of Israel.

31. But for all this they sinned yet more:
    and put no faith in his wonders.

32. So he ended their days like a breath:
    and their years with sudden terror.

33. When he struck them down, then they sought him:
    they turned, and sought eagerly for God.

34. They remembered that God was their rock:
    that God Most High was their redeemer.

35. But they lied to him with their mouths:
    and dissembled with their tongues;

36. For their hearts were not fixed upon him:
    nor were they true to his covenant.

37. Yet he, being merciful, forgave their iniquity
       and did not destroy them:
    many times he turned his anger aside,
       and would not wholly arouse his fury.

38. He remembered that they were but flesh:
    like a wind that passes, and does not return.

39. How often they rebelled against him in the wilderness:
    and grieved him in the desert!

40. Again and again they put God to the test:
    and provoked the Holy One of Israel.

41. They did not remember his power:
    or the day when he redeemed them from the enemy;

42. How he wrought his signs in Egypt:
    his wonders in the country of Zoan.

43. For he turned their rivers into blood:
     so that they could not drink from the streams.

44. He sent swarms of flies that devoured them:
     and frogs that laid them waste.

45. He gave their crops to the locust:
     and the fruits of their labour to the grasshopper.

46. He struck down their vines with hailstones:
     and their sycomore trees with frost.

47. He gave up their cattle to the hail:
     and their flocks to the flash of the lightning.

48. He loosed on them the fierceness of his anger,
      his fury, his indignation and distress:
    and these were his messengers of destruction.

49. He opened a path for his fury:
     he would not spare them from death,
    but gave up their lives to the pestilence.

50. He struck down the firstborn of Egypt:
     the first-fruits of their manhood
    in the dwellings of Ham.

51. As for his own people, he led them out like sheep:
     and guided them in the wilderness like a flock.

52. He led them in safety, and they were not afraid:
     but the sea covered their enemies.

53. He brought them to his holy land:
     to the mountains that his own right hand had won.

54. He drove out the nations before them,
      and apportioned their lands as a possession:
    and settled the tribes of Israel in their tents.

55. But they rebelled against God Most High
      and put him to the test:
    they would not obey his commandments.

56. They turned back and dealt treacherously
      like their fathers:
    they turned aside, slack as an unstrung bow.

57. They provoked him to anger with their heathen shrines:
    and moved him to jealousy with their carved images.
58. God heard and was angry, he utterly rejected Israel:
    he forsook the tabernacle at Shiloh,
    the tent where he dwelt among men.
59. He gave the ark of his might into captivity:
    and his glory into the hands of the enemy.
60. He delivered his people to the sword:
    and was enraged against his own possession.
61. Fire devoured the young men:
    there was no one to bewail the maidens;
62. Their priests fell by the sword:
    and there was none to mourn for the widows.
63. Then the Lord awoke like a man out of sleep:
    like a warrior that had been overcome with wine.
64. He struck the backs of his enemies as they fled:
    and put them to perpetual shame.
65. He rejected the family of Joseph:
    he refused the tribe of Ephraim.
66. But he chose the tribe of Judah:
    and the hill of Zion which he loved.
67. He built his sanctuary like the heights of heaven:
    like the earth which he had founded for ever.
68. He chose David his servant:
    and took him from the sheepfolds;
69. He brought him from following the ewes:
    to be the shepherd of his people Jacob,
    and of Israel his own possession.
70. So he tended them with upright heart:
    and guided them with skilful hand.

Psalm 79

1. O God, the heathen have come into your land:
    they have defiled your holy temple,
   they have made Jerusalem a heap of stones.

2. They have given the dead bodies of your servants
    as food to the birds of the air:
   and the flesh of your faithful ones
    to the wild beasts of the earth.

3. Their blood they have spilt like water
    on every side of Jerusalem:
   and there is none to bury them.

4. We have become a mockery to our neighbours:
    the scorn and laughing-stock of those about us.

5. How long, O Lord, shall your anger be so extreme:
    will your jealous fury burn like fire?

6. Pour out your wrath on the nations that do not know you:
    on the kingdoms that have not called upon your name.

7. For they have devoured Jacob:
    and made his dwelling-place a desolation.

8. Do not remember against us the sin of former times:
    but let your compassion hasten to meet us,
   for we are brought very low.

9. Help us, O God our saviour,
    for the honour of your name:
   O deliver us and expiate our sins, for your name's sake.

10. [Why should the heathen say 'Where is their God?':
    O let vengeance for the blood of your servants that is shed
   be shown upon the nations in our sight.]

11. Let the sorrowful sighing of the prisoners
    come before you:
   and as your power is great,
    reprieve those condemned to die.

12. [For the taunts with which our neighbours
        have taunted you, O Lord:
    repay them seven times over into their bosoms.]

13. So we that are your people and the sheep of your pasture
        shall give you thanks for ever:
    we will declare your praise in every generation.

Psalm 80

1. Hear, O Shepherd of Israel,
        you that led Joseph like a flock:
    you that are enthroned upon the cherubim,
        shine out in glory;

2. Before Ephraim, Benjamin and Manasseh:
        stir up your power, and come to save us.

3. *Restore us again, O Lord of hosts:*
        show us the light of your countenance,
    and we shall be saved.

4. O Lord God of hosts:
        how long will you be angry at your people's prayer?

5. You have fed them with the bread of tears:
        and given them tears to drink in good measure.

6. You have made us the victim of our neighbours:
        and our enemies laugh us to scorn.

7. *Restore us again, O Lord of hosts:*
        show us the light of your countenance,
    and we shall be saved.

8. You brought a vine out of Egypt:
        you drove out the nations, and planted it in.

9. You cleared the ground before it:
        and it struck root and filled the land.

10. The hills were covered with its shadow:
        and its boughs were like the boughs of the great cedars.

11. It stretched out its branches to the sea:
     and its tender shoots to the Great River.

12. Why then have you broken down its walls:
     so that every passer-by can pluck its fruit?

13. The wild boar out of the woods roots it up:
     and the locusts from the wild places devour it.

14. Turn to us again, O Lord of hosts:
     look down from heaven, and see.

15. Bestow your care upon this vine:
     the stock which your own right hand has planted.

16. As for those that burn it with fire and cut it down:
     let them perish at the rebuke of your countenance.

17. Let your power rest on the man at your right hand:
     on that son of man whom you made so strong for yourself.

18. And so we shall not turn back from you:
     give us life, and we will call upon your name.

19. *Restore us again, O Lord of hosts:*
     show us the light of your countenance,
 and we shall be saved.

Psalm 81

1. O sing joyfully to God our strength:
     shout in triumph to the God of Jacob.

2. Make music and beat upon the drum:
     sound the lute and the melodious harp.

3. Blow the ram's horn at the new moon:
     and at the full moon of our day of festival.

4. For this was a statute for Israel:
     a commandment of the God of Jacob,

5. Which he laid on Joseph as a solemn charge:
     when he came out of the land of Egypt.

6. I heard a voice that I had not known, saying:
      'I eased your shoulders of the burden,
   and your hands were freed from the load.

7. 'You called to me in trouble, and I rescued you:
      I answered you from the secret place of my thunder,
   I put you to the test at the waters of Meribah.

8. 'Listen, my people, and I will admonish you:
      O Israel, if only you would hear me.

9. 'There shall be no strange god among you:
      nor shall you bow down to an alien god.

10. 'I am the Lord your God,
       who brought you up from the land of Egypt:
    open wide your mouth, and I will fill it.

11. 'But my people would not listen to my voice:
       and Israel would have none of me.

12. 'So I left them to the stubbornness of their hearts:
       to walk according to their own designs.

13. 'If only my people would listen:
       if Israel would but walk in my ways,

14. 'I would soon put down their enemies:
       and turn my hand against their adversaries.

15. 'Those that hate the Lord would cringe before him:
       and their punishment would last for ever.

16. 'But Israel I would feed with the finest wheat:
       and satisfy you with honey from the rocks.'

Psalm 82

1. God has stood up in the council of heaven:
      in the midst of the gods he gives judgement.

2. 'How long will you judge unjustly:
      and favour the cause of the wicked?

3. 'Judge for the poor and fatherless:
      vindicate the afflicted and oppressed.

4. 'Rescue the poor and needy:
     and save them from the hands of the wicked.

5. 'They do not know, they do not understand,
     they walk about in darkness:
   all the foundations of the earth are shaken.

6. 'Therefore I say, "Though you are gods:
     and all of you sons of the Most High,

7. '"Nevertheless you shall die like man:
     and fall like one of the princes."'

8. Arise, O God, and judge the earth:
     for you shall take all nations as your possession.

Psalm 83

1. Hold not your peace, O God:
     O God, be not silent or unmoved.

2. See how your enemies make uproar:
     how those that hate you have lifted up their heads.

3. For they lay shrewd plots against your people:
     they scheme against those whom you have cherished.

4. 'Come', they say, 'let us destroy them,
       that they may no longer be a nation:
   that the very name of Israel
       may be remembered no more.'

5. With one mind they conspire together:
     they make alliance against you,

6. The tribes of Edom and the Ishmaelites:
     the people of Moab and the Hagarites,

7. Gebal and Ammon and Amalek:
     Philistia, and the inhabitants of Tyre;

8. Asshur also is joined with them:
     and lends a friendly arm to the children of Lot.

9. Do to them as you did to Midian:
     as to Sisera and Jabin at the river of Kishon,

10. Who were destroyed at Endor:
    and became like dung for the earth.

11. Make their leaders as Oreb and Zeeb:
    and all their princes like Zebah and Zalmunna,

12. Who said 'Let us take possession:
    let us seize the pastures of God'.

13. Make them like thistledown, my God:
    or like chaff blown before the wind.

14. As fire consuming a thicket:
    or as flame that sets the hillsides ablaze,

15. Pursue them with your tempest:
    and terrify them with your storm-wind.

16. Cover their faces with shame, O Lord:
    that they may seek your name.

17. [Let them be disgraced and dismayed for ever:
    let them be confounded and perish,]

18. That they may know that you, whose name is the Lord:
    are alone the Most High over all the earth.

Psalm 84

1. How lovely is your dwelling-place:
   O Lord God of hosts!

2. My soul has a desire and longing
      to enter the courts of the Lord:
   my heart and my flesh rejoice in the living God.

3. The sparrow has found her a home,
      and the swallow a nest where she may lay her young:
   even your altar, O Lord of hosts, my King and my God.

4. Blessed are those who dwell in your house:
   they will always be praising you.

5. Blessed is the man whose strength is in you:
   in whose heart are the highways to Zion.

6. Who, going through the valley of dryness,
     finds there a spring from which to drink:
   till the autumn rain shall clothe it with blessings.

7. They go from strength to strength:
     they appear, every one of them,
   before the God of gods in Zion.

8. O Lord God of hosts, hear my prayer:
     give ear, O God of Jacob.

9. Behold, O God, him who reigns over us:
     and look upon the face of your anointed.

10. One day in your courts is better than a thousand:
      I would rather stand at the threshold
    of the house of my God
      than dwell in the tents of ungodliness.

11. For the Lord God is a rampart and a shield,
      the Lord gives favour and honour:
    and no good thing will he withhold
      from those who walk in innocence.

12. O Lord God of hosts:
      blessed is the man who puts his trust in you.

Psalm 85

1. O Lord, you were gracious to your land:
     you restored the fortunes of Jacob.

2. You forgave the iniquity of your people:
     and covered all their sin.

3. You put aside all your wrath:
     and turned away from your fierce indignation.

4. Return to us again, O God our saviour:
     and let your anger cease from us.

5. Will you be displeased with us for ever:
     will you stretch out your wrath
   from one generation to another?

6. Will you not give us life again:
    that your people may rejoice in you?

7. Show us your mercy, O Lord:
    and grant us your salvation.

8. I will hear what the Lord God will speak:
    for he will speak peace to his people,
   to his faithful ones, whose hearts are turned to him.

9. Truly his salvation is near to those that fear him:
    and his glory shall dwell in our land.

10. Mercy and truth are met together:
    righteousness and peace have kissed each other;

11. Truth shall flourish out of the earth:
    and righteousness shall look down from heaven.

12. The Lord will also give us all that is good:
    and our land shall yield its plenty.

13. For righteousness shall go before him:
    and tread the path before his feet.

Psalm 86

1. Incline your ear to me, O God, and answer me:
    for I am poor and in misery.

2. Preserve my life, for I am faithful:
    My God, save your servant who puts his trust in you.

3. Be merciful to me, O Lord:
    for I call to you all the day long.

4. O make glad the soul of your servant:
    for I put my hope in you, O Lord.

5. For you, Lord, are good and forgiving:
    of great and continuing kindness
   to all who call upon you.

6. Hear my prayer, O Lord:
    and give heed to the voice of my supplication.

7. In the day of my trouble I call upon you:
   for you will surely answer.

8. Among the gods there is none like you, O Lord:
   nor are there any deeds like yours.

9. All the nations you have made
     shall come and worship before you:
   O Lord, they shall glorify your name.

10. For you are great and do marvellous things:
    and you alone are God.

11. Show me your way, O Lord, and I will walk in your truth:
    let my heart delight to fear your name.

12. I will praise you, O Lord my God, with all my heart:
    and I will glorify your name for ever.

13. For great is your abiding love toward me:
      and you have delivered my life
    from the lowest depths of the grave.

14. Insolent men, O God, have risen against me:
      a band of ruthless men seek my life,
    they have not set God before their eyes.

15. But you, Lord, are a God gracious and compassionate:
    slow to anger, full of goodness and truth.

16. Turn to me and be merciful,
      give your strength to your servant:
    and save the son of your handmaid.

17. Show me some token of your goodness:
      that those who hate me may see it and be ashamed,
    because you, Lord, are my helper and my comforter.

Psalm 87

1. He has founded it upon a holy hill:
     and the Lord loves the gates of Zion
   more than all the dwellings of Jacob.

2. Glorious things shall be spoken of you:
   O Zion, city of our God.

3. I might speak of my kinsmen in Egypt or in Babylon:
   in Philistia, Tyre or Nubia, where each was born.

4. But of Zion it shall be said:
   many were born in her,
   he that is Most High has established her.

5. When the Lord draws up the record of the nations:
   he shall take note where every man was born.

6. And the singers and the dancers together:
   shall make their song to your name.

Psalm 88

1. O Lord my God, I call for help by day:
   and by night also I cry out before you.

2. Let my prayer come into your presence:
   and turn your ear to my loud crying.

3. For my soul is filled with trouble:
   and my life has come even to the brink of the grave.

4. I am reckoned among those that go down to the Pit:
   I am a man that has no help.

5. I lie among the dead,
      like the slain that sleep in the grave:
   whom you remember no more,
      who are cut off from your power.

6. You have laid me in the lowest Pit:
   in darkness and in the watery depths.

7. Your wrath lies heavy upon me:
   and all your waves are brought against me.

8. You have put my friends far from me:
   and made me to be abhorred by them.

9. I am so fast in prison I cannot get free:
   my eyes fail because of my affliction.

10. Lord, I call to you every day:
    I stretch out my hands toward you.

11. Will you work wonders for the dead:
    or will the shades rise up again to praise you?

12. Shall your love be declared in the grave:
    or your faithfulness in the place of destruction?

13. Will your wonders be made known in the dark:
    or your righteousness
    in the land where all things are forgotten?

14. But to you, Lord, will I cry:
    early in the morning my prayer shall come before you.

15. O Lord, why have you rejected me:
    why do you hide your face from me?

16. I have been afflicted and wearied from my youth upward:
    I am tossed high and low, I cease to be.

17. Your fierce anger has overwhelmed me:
    and your terrors have put me to silence.

18. They surround me like a flood all the day long:
    they close upon me from every side.

19. Friend and acquaintance you have put far from me:
    and kept my companions from my sight.

Psalm 89

1. Lord, I will sing for ever of your loving-kindnesses:
    my mouth shall proclaim your faithfulness
    throughout all generations.

2. I have said of your loving-kindness
    that it is built for ever:
    you have established your faithfulness in the heavens.

3. The Lord said 'I have made a covenant with my chosen:
    I have sworn an oath to my servant David.

4. 'I will establish your line for ever:
    and build up your throne for all generations.'

5. Let the heavens praise your wonders, O Lord:
    and let your faithfulness be sung
    in the assembly of the holy ones.

6. For who amidst the clouds can be compared to the Lord:
   or who is like the Lord among the sons of heaven?

7. —A God to be feared in the council of the holy ones:
   great and terrible above all that are around him.

8. O Lord God of hosts, who is like you?:
   your power and your faithfulness are all about you.

9. You rule the raging of the sea:
   when its waves surge, you still them.

10. You crushed Rahab like a carcase:
    you scattered your enemies by your mighty arm.

11. The heavens are yours, so also is the earth:
    you founded the world and all that is in it.

12. You created the north and the south:
    Tabor and Mount Hermon shall sing of your name.

13. Mighty is your arm:
    strong is your hand, and your right hand is lifted high.

14. Righteousness and justice
      are the foundation of your throne:
    loving-kindness and faithfulness attend your presence.

15. Happy the people who know the triumphal shout:
    who walk, O Lord, in the light of your countenance.

16. They rejoice all the day long because of your name:
    because of your righteousness they are exalted.

17. For you are their glory and their strength:
    and our heads are uplifted by your favour.

18. Our king belongs to the Lord:
    he that rules over us to the Holy One of Israel.

19. You spoke once in a vision:
    and said to your faithful one,

20. 'I have set a youth above a warrior:
    I have exalted a young man out of the people.

21. 'I have found my servant David:
    and anointed him with my holy oil.

22. 'My hand shall uphold him:
    and my arm shall strengthen him.

23. 'No enemy shall deceive him:
    no evil man shall hurt him.

24. 'I will crush his adversaries before him:
    and strike down those that hate him.

25. 'My faithfulness and loving-kindness shall be with him:
    and through my name his head shall be lifted high.

26. 'I will set the hand of his dominion
       upon the Western Sea:
    and his right hand shall stretch
       to the streams of Mesopotamia.

27. 'He will call to me "You are my Father:
    my God, and the Rock of my salvation".

28. 'I will make him my first-born son:
    and highest among the kings of the earth.

29. 'I will ever maintain my loving-kindness toward him:
    and my covenant with him shall stand firm.

30. 'I will establish his line for ever:
    and his throne like the days of heaven.

31. 'If his children forsake my law:
    and will not walk in my judgements;

32. 'If they profane my statutes:
    and do not keep my commandments,

33. 'Then I will punish their rebellion with the rod:
    and their iniquity with blows.

34. 'But I will not cause my loving-kindness
       to cease from him:
    nor will I betray my faithfulness.

35. 'I will not profane my covenant:
    or alter what has passed from my lips.

36. 'Once and for all I have sworn by my holiness:
      I will not prove false to David.

37. 'His posterity shall endure for ever:
      and his throne be as the sun before me;

38. 'Like the moon that is established for ever:
      and stands in the heavens for evermore.'

39. Yet you have been enraged against your anointed:
      you have abhorred him and rejected him.

40. You have spurned the covenant with your servant:
      and defiled his crown to the dust.

41. You have broken down all his walls:
      and made his strongholds desolate.

42. All that pass by plunder him:
      he has become the scorn of his neighbours.

43. You have exalted the right hand of his adversaries:
      and gladdened all his enemies.

44. His bright sword you have turned backward:
      you have not enabled him to stand in the battle.

45. You have brought his lustre to an end:
      you have cast his throne to the ground.

46. You have cut short the days of his youth:
      and clothed him with dishonour.

47. How long, O Lord, will you hide yourself so utterly:
      how long shall your fury burn like fire?

48. Remember how I draw to my eternal end:
      have you created all mankind for nothing?

49. Where is the man who can live and not see death?:
      who can deliver his life from the power of the grave?

50. Where, O Lord, are your loving-kindnesses of old:
      which you have vowed to David in your faithfulness?

51. Remember, O Lord, how your servant is reviled:
      how I bear in my bosom the onslaught of the peoples;

52. Remember how your enemies taunt:
    how they mock the footsteps of your anointed.

53. Blessed be the Lord for ever:
    Amen and amen.

Psalm 90

1. Lord, you have been our refuge:
   from one generation to another.

2. Before the mountains were born
     or the earth and the world were brought to be:
   from eternity to eternity you are God.

3. You turn man back into dust:
   saying 'Return to dust, you sons of Adam'.

4. For a thousand years in your sight
     are like yesterday passing:
   or like one watch of the night.

5. You cut them short like a dream:
   like the fresh grass of the morning;

6. In the morning it is green and flourishes:
   at evening it is withered and dried up.

7. And we are consumed by your anger:
   because of your indignation we cease to be.

8. You have brought our iniquities before you:
   and our secret sins to the light of your countenance.

9. Our days decline beneath your wrath:
   and our years pass away like a sigh.

10. The days of our life are three score years and ten,
      or if we have strength, four score:
    the pride of our labours is but toil and sorrow,
      for it passes quickly away and we are gone.

11. Who can know the power of your wrath:
    who can know your indignation like those that fear you?

12. Teach us so to number our days:
    that we may apply our hearts to wisdom.

13. Relent, O Lord; how long will you be angry?:
    take pity on your servants.

14. O satisfy us early with your mercy:
    that all our days we may rejoice and sing.

15. Give us joy for all the days you have afflicted us:
    for the years we have suffered adversity.

16. Show your servants your work:
    and let their children see your glory.

17. May the gracious favour of the Lord our God be upon us:
    prosper the work of our hands,
    O prosper the work of our hands!

Psalm 91

1. He who dwells in the shelter of the Most High:
   who abides under the shadow of the Almighty,

2. He will say to the Lord
   'You are my refuge and my stronghold:
   my God in whom I trust'.

3. For he will deliver you from the snare of the hunter:
   and from the destroying curse.

4. He will cover you with his wings,
   and you will be safe under his feathers:
   his faithfulness will be your shield and defence.

5. You shall not be afraid of any terror by night:
   or of the arrow that flies by day,

6. Of the pestilence that walks about in darkness:
   or the plague that destroys at noonday.

7. A thousand may fall beside you,
   and ten thousand at your right hand:
   but you it shall not touch;

8. Your own eyes shall see:
      and look on the reward of the ungodly.

9. The Lord himself is your refuge:
      you have made the Most High your stronghold.

10. Therefore no harm will befall you:
      nor will any scourge come near your tent.

11. For he will command his angels:
      to keep you in all your ways.

12. They will bear you up in their hands:
      lest you dash your foot against a stone.

13. You will tread on the lion and the adder:
      the young lion and the serpent
    you will trample under foot.

14. 'He has set his love upon me,
      and therefore I will deliver him:
    I will lift him out of danger,
      because he has known my name.

15. 'When he calls upon me I will answer him:
      I will be with him in trouble,
    I will rescue him and bring him to honour.

16. 'With long life I will satisfy him:
      and fill him with my salvation.'

Psalm 92

1. How good to give thanks to the Lord:
      to sing praises to your name, O Most High,

2. To declare your love in the morning:
      and at night to sing of your faithfulness,

3. Upon the lute, upon the lute of ten strings:
      and to the melody of the lyre.

4. For in all you have done, O Lord, you have made me glad:
      I will sing for joy because of the works of your hands.

5. Lord, how glorious are your works:
    your thoughts are very deep.

6. The brutish do not consider:
    and the fool cannot understand

7. That though the wicked sprout like grass:
    and all wrongdoers flourish,

8. They flourish to be destroyed for ever:
    but you, Lord, are exalted for evermore.

9. For behold, your enemies, O Lord,
    your enemies shall perish:
   and all the workers of wickedness shall be scattered.

10. You have lifted up my head
    like the horns of the wild oxen:
    I am anointed with fresh oil;

11. My eyes have looked down on my enemies:
    and my ears have heard the ruin
    of those who rose up against me.

12. The righteous shall flourish like the palm tree:
    they shall spread abroad like a cedar in Lebanon;

13. For they are planted in the house of the Lord:
    and flourish in the courts of our God.

14. In old age they shall be full of sap:
    they shall be sturdy and laden with branches;

15. And they will say that the Lord is just:
    the Lord my Rock, in whom is no unrighteousness.

Psalm 93

1. The Lord is king, and has put on robes of glory:
    the Lord has put on his glory,
   he has girded himself with strength.

2. He has made the world so firm:
    that it cannot be moved.

3. Your throne is established from of old:
    you are from everlasting.

4. The floods have lifted up, O Lord,
    the floods have lifted up their voice:
   the floods lift up their pounding.

5. But mightier than the sound of many waters,
    than the mighty waters or the breakers of the sea:
   the Lord on high is mighty.

6. Your decrees are very sure:
    and holiness, O Lord, adorns your house for ever.

Psalm 94

1. O Lord God to whom vengeance belongs:
    O God to whom vengeance belongs, shine out in glory.

2. Arise, judge of the earth:
    and requite the proud as they deserve.

3. Lord, how long shall the wicked:
    how long shall the wicked triumph?

4. How long shall all evildoers pour out words:
    how long shall they boast and flaunt themselves?

5. They crush your people, O Lord:
    they oppress your own possession.

6. They murder the widow and the alien:
    they put the fatherless to death.

7. And they say 'The Lord does not see:
    nor does the God of Jacob consider it'.

8. Consider this, you senseless among the people:
    fools, when will you understand?

9. He who planted the ear, does he not hear:
    he who formed the eye, does he not see?

10. He who disciplines the nations, will he not punish:
    has the teacher of mankind no knowledge?

11. The Lord knows the thoughts of man:
    he knows that they are mere breath.

12. Blessed is the man whom you discipline, O Lord:
    and teach from your law,

13. Giving him rest from days of misery:
    till a pit is dug for the wicked.

14. The Lord will not cast off his people:
    nor will he forsake his own.

15. For justice shall return to the righteous man:
    and, with him, to all the true of heart.

16. Who will stand up for me against the wicked:
    who will take my part against the evildoers?

17. If the Lord had not been my helper:
    I would soon have dwelt in the land of silence.

18. But when I said 'My foot has slipped':
    your mercy, O Lord, was holding me.

19. In all the doubts of my heart:
    your consolations delighted my soul.

20. Will you be any friend to the court of wickedness:
    that contrives evil by means of law?

21. They band together against the life of the righteous:
    and condemn innocent blood.

22. But the Lord is my stronghold:
    my God is my rock and my refuge.

23. Let him requite them for their wickedness,
    and silence them for their evil:
    the Lord our God shall silence them.

Psalm 95

1. O come, let us sing out to the Lord:
   let us shout in triumph to the rock of our salvation.

2. Let us come before his face with thanksgiving:
   and cry out to him joyfully in psalms.

3. For the Lord is a great God:
   and a great king above all gods.

4. In his hand are the depths of the earth:
   and the peaks of the mountains are his also.

5. The sea is his and he made it:
   his hands moulded dry land.

6. Come, let us worship and bow down:
   and kneel before the Lord our maker.

7. For he is the Lord our God:
   we are his people and the sheep of his pasture.

8. Today if only you would hear his voice—
   'Do not harden your hearts as at Meribah:
   as on that day at Massah in the wilderness;

9. 'When your fathers tested me:
   put me to proof, though they had seen my works.

10. 'Forty years long I loathed that generation and said:
    "It is a people who err in their hearts,
    for they do not know my ways";

11. 'Of whom I swore in my wrath:
    "They shall not enter my rest."'

Psalm 96

1. O sing to the Lord a new song:
   sing to the Lord, all the earth.

2. Sing to the Lord and bless his holy name:
   proclaim the good news of his salvation from day to day.

3. Declare his glory among the nations:
   and his wonders among all peoples.

4. For great is the Lord, and greatly to be praised:
   he is more to be feared than all gods.

5. As for all the gods of the nations, they are mere idols:
    it is the Lord who made the heavens.

6. Majesty and glory are before him:
    beauty and power are in his sanctuary.

7. Render to the Lord, you families of the nations:
    render to the Lord glory and might.

8. Render to the Lord the honour due to his name:
    bring offerings and come into his courts.

9. O worship the Lord in the beauty of his holiness:
    let the whole earth stand in awe of him.

10. Say among the nations that the Lord is king:
    he has made the world so firm that it can never be moved;
    and he shall judge the peoples with equity.

11. Let the heavens rejoice and let the earth be glad:
    let the sea roar, and all that fills it:

12. Let the fields rejoice, and everything in them:
    then shall all the trees of the wood
    shout with joy before the Lord;

13. For he comes, he comes to judge the earth:
    he shall judge the world with righteousness,
    and the peoples with his truth.

Psalm 97

1. The Lord is king; let the earth rejoice:
    let the multitude of islands be glad.

2. Clouds and darkness are round about him:
    righteousness and justice are the foundation of his throne.

3. Fire goes before him:
    and burns up his enemies on every side.

4. His lightnings light the world:
    the earth sees it and quakes.

5. The mountains melt like wax before his face:
    from before the face of the Lord of all the earth.

6. The heavens have proclaimed his righteousness:
    and all peoples have seen his glory.

7. They are ashamed,
    all those who serve idols and glory in mere nothings:
   all gods bow down before him.

8. Zion heard and was glad,
    and the daughters of Judah rejoiced:
   because of your judgements, O God.

9. For you, Lord, are most high over all the earth:
    you are exalted far above all gods.

10. The Lord loves those that hate evil:
     the Lord guards the life of the faithful,
     and delivers them from the hand of the ungodly.

11. Light dawns for the righteous:
     and joy for the true of heart.

12. Rejoice in the Lord, you righteous:
     and give thanks to his holy name.

Psalm 98

1. O sing to the Lord a new song:
    for he has done marvellous things;

2. His right hand and his holy arm:
    they have got him the victory.

3. The Lord has made known his salvation:
    he has revealed his just deliverance
   in the sight of the nations.

4. He has remembered his mercy and faithfulness
      towards the house of Israel:
   and all the ends of the earth
      have seen the salvation of our God.

5. Shout with joy to the Lord, all the earth:
    break into singing and make melody.

6. Make melody to the Lord upon the harp:
    upon the harp and with the sounds of praise.

7. With trumpets and with horns:
    cry out in triumph before the Lord, the king.

8. Let the sea roar, and all that fills it:
    the good earth and those who live upon it.

9. Let the rivers clap their hands:
    and let the mountains ring out together before the Lord;

10. For he comes to judge the earth:
    he shall judge the world with righteousness,
    and the peoples with equity.

Psalm 99

1. The Lord is king, let the nations tremble:
    he is enthroned upon the cherubim; let the earth quake.

2. The Lord is great in Zion:
    he is high above all nations.

3. Let them praise your great and terrible name:
    for holy is the Lord.

4. The Mighty One is king and loves justice:
    you have established equity,
    you have dealt righteousness and justice in Jacob.

5. *O exalt the Lord our God:*
    and bow down before his footstool, for he is holy.

6. Moses and Aaron among his priests,
    and Samuel among those who call upon his name:
    they called to the Lord and he answered.

7. He spoke to them from the pillar of cloud:
    they kept to his teachings and the law that he gave them.

8. You answered them, O Lord our God:
      you were a forgiving God to them,
   and pardoned their wrongdoing.

9. *O exalt the Lord our God:*
      and bow down towards his holy hill,
   for the Lord our God is holy.

Psalm 100

1. O shout to the Lord in triumph, all the earth:
      serve the Lord with gladness,
   and come before his face with songs of joy.

2. Know that the Lord he is God:
      it is he who has made us and we are his;
   we are his people and the sheep of his pasture.

3. Come into his gates with thanksgiving,
      and into his courts with praise:
   give thanks to him, and bless his holy name.

4. For the Lord is good, his loving mercy is for ever:
      his faithfulness throughout all generations.

Psalm 101

1. My song shall be of steadfastness and justice:
      to you, Lord, will I sing.

2. I will be wise in the way of innocence:
      O when will you come to me?

3. I will walk within my house:
      in purity of heart.

4. I will set nothing evil before my eyes:
      I hate the sin of backsliders, it shall get no hold on me.

5. Crookedness of heart shall depart from me:
      I will know nothing of wickedness.

6. [The man who secretly slanders his neighbour
        I will destroy:
    the proud look and the arrogant heart I will not endure.]

7. My eyes shall look to the faithful in the land,
        and they shall make their home with me:
    one who walks in the way of innocence,
        he shall minister to me.

8. No man who practises deceit shall live in my house:
        no one who utters lies shall stand in my sight.

9. [Morning by morning I will destroy
        all the wicked of the land:
    and cut off all evildoers from the city of the Lord.]

Psalm 102

1. O Lord, hear my prayer:
        and let my cry come to you.

2. Do not hide your face from me in the day of my trouble:
        turn your ear to me;
    and when I call, be swift to answer.

3. For my days pass away like smoke:
        and my bones burn as in a furnace.

4. My heart is scorched and withered like grass:
        and I forget to eat my bread.

5. I am weary with the sound of my groaning:
        my bones stick fast to my skin.

6. I have become like an owl in the wilderness:
        like a screech owl among the ruins.

7. I keep watch and flit to and fro:
        like a sparrow upon a housetop.

8. My enemies taunt me all day long:
        and those who rave at me make oaths against me.

9. Surely I have eaten ashes for bread:
        and mingled my drink with tears,

10. Because of your wrath and indignation:
    for you have taken me up and tossed me aside.

11. My days decline like a shadow:
    and I wither away like grass.

12. But you, Lord, are enthroned for ever:
    and your name shall be known throughout all generations.

13. You will arise and have mercy upon Zion:
    for it is time to pity her, the appointed time has come.

14. Your servants love even her stones:
    and her dust moves them to pity.

15. Then shall the nations fear your name, O Lord:
    and all the kings of the earth your glory,

16. When the Lord has built up Zion:
    when he shows himself in his glory,

17. When he turns to the prayer of the destitute:
    and does not despise their supplication.

18. Let this be written down for those who come after:
    and a people yet unborn will praise the Lord.

19. For the Lord has looked down
      from the height of his holiness:
    from heaven he has looked upon the earth,

20. To hear the groaning of the prisoner:
    to deliver those condemned to die;

21. That they may proclaim the name of the Lord in Zion:
    and his praises in Jerusalem,

22. When the nations are gathered together:
    and the kingdoms, to serve the Lord.

23. He has broken my strength before my time:
    he has cut short my days.

24. Do not take me away, O God, in the midst of my life:
    you, whose years extend through all generations.

25. In the beginning you laid the foundations of the earth:
    and the heavens are the work of your hands.

26. They shall perish, but you will endure:
     they shall all grow old like a garment;
    like clothes you will change them,
     and they shall pass away.

27. But you are the same for ever:
     and your years will never fail.

28. The children of your servants shall rest secure:
     and their seed shall be established in your sight.

Psalm 103

1. Praise the Lord, O my soul:
    and all that is within me, praise his holy name.

2. Praise the Lord, O my soul:
    and forget not all his benefits,

3. Who forgives all your sin:
    and heals all your infirmities,

4. Who redeems your life from the Pit:
    and crowns you with mercy and compassion;

5. Who satisfies your being with good things:
    so that your youth is renewed like an eagle's.

6. The Lord works righteousness:
    and justice for all who are oppressed.

7. He made known his ways to Moses:
    and his works to the children of Israel.

8. The Lord is full of compassion and mercy:
    slow to anger and of great goodness.

9. He will not always be chiding:
    nor will he keep his anger for ever.

10. He has not dealt with us according to our sins:
     nor rewarded us according to our wickedness.

11. For as the heavens are high above the earth:
     so great is his mercy over those that fear him;

12. As far as the east is from the west:
    so far has he set our sins from us.

13. As a father is tender towards his children:
    so is the Lord tender to those that fear him.

14. For he knows of what we are made:
    he remembers that we are but dust.

15. The days of man are but as grass:
    he flourishes like a flower of the field;

16. When the wind goes over it, it is gone:
    and its place will know it no more.

17. But the merciful goodness of the Lord
      endures for ever and ever toward those that fear him:
    and his righteousness upon their children's children;

18. Upon those who keep his covenant:
    and remember his commandments to do them.

19. The Lord has established his throne in heaven:
    and his kingdom rules over all.

20. Praise the Lord, all you his angels,
      you that excel in strength:
    you that fulfil his word,
      and obey the voice of his commandment.

21. Praise the Lord, all you his hosts:
    his servants who do his will.

22. Praise the Lord, all his works,
      in all places of his dominion:
    praise the Lord, O my soul!

Psalm 104

1. Bless the Lord, O my soul:
   O Lord my God, how great you are!

2. Clothed with majesty and honour:
   wrapped in light as in a garment.

3. You have stretched out the heavens like a tent-cloth:
    and laid the beams of your dwelling upon their waters;
4. You make the clouds your chariot:
    and ride upon the wings of the wind;
5. You make the winds your messengers:
    and flames of fire your ministers;
6. You have set the earth on its foundations:
    so that it shall never be moved.
7. The deep covered it as with a mantle:
    the waters stood above the hills.
8. At your rebuke they fled:
    at the voice of your thunder they hurried away;
9. They went up to the mountains,
        they went down by the valleys:
    to the place which you had appointed for them.
10. You fixed a limit which they may not pass:
    they shall not return again to cover the earth.
11. You send springs into the gullies:
    which run between the hills;
12. They give drink to every beast of the field:
    and the wild asses quench their thirst.
13. Beside them the birds of the air build their nests:
    and sing among the branches.
14. You water the mountains from your dwelling on high:
    and the earth is filled by the fruits of your work.
15. You cause the grass to grow for the cattle:
    and all green things for the servants of mankind.
16. You bring food out of the earth:
    and wine that makes glad the heart of man,
17. Oil to give him a shining countenance:
    and bread to strengthen his heart.
18. The trees of the Lord are well-watered:
    the cedars of Lebanon that he has planted,

19. Where the birds build their nests:
    and the stork makes her home in the pine-tops.

20. The high hills are a refuge for the wild goats:
    and the crags a cover for the conies.

21. You created the moon to mark the seasons:
    and the sun knows the hour of its setting.

22. You make darkness, and it is night:
    in which all the beasts of the forest move by stealth.

23. The lions roar for their prey:
    seeking their food from God.

24. When the sun rises, they retire:
    and lay themselves down in their dens.

25. Man goes out to his work:
    and to his labour until the evening.

26. Lord, how various are your works:
    in wisdom you have made them all,
    and the earth is full of your creatures.

27. There is the wide, immeasurable sea:
    there move living things without number, great and small;

28. There go the ships, to and fro:
    and there is that Leviathan
    whom you formed to sport in the deep.

29. These all look to you:
    to give them their food in due season.

30. When you give it to them, they gather it:
    when you open your hand
    they are satisfied with good things.

31. When you hide your face, they are troubled:
    when you take away their breath,
    they die and return to their dust.

32. When you send forth your spirit they are created:
    and you renew the face of the earth.

33. May the glory of the Lord endure for ever:
    may the Lord rejoice in his works.

34. If he look upon the earth, it shall tremble:
    if he but touch the mountains, they shall smoke.

35. I will sing to the Lord as long as I live:
    I will praise my God while I have any being.

36. May my meditation be pleasing to him:
    for my joy shall be in the Lord.

37. May sinners perish from the earth,
    let the wicked be no more:
    bless the Lord, O my soul; O praise the Lord.

Psalm 105

1. O give thanks to the Lord and call upon his name:
   tell among the peoples what things he has done.

2. Sing to him, O sing praises:
   and be telling of all his marvellous works.

3. Exult in his holy name:
   and let those that seek the Lord be joyful in heart.

4. Seek the Lord and his strength:
   O seek his face continually.

5. Call to mind what wonders he has done:
   his marvellous acts, and the judgements of his mouth,

6. O seed of Abraham his servant:
   O children of Jacob his chosen one.

7. For he is the Lord our God:
   and his judgements are in all the earth.

8. He has remembered his covenant for ever:
   the word that he ordained for a thousand generations,

9. The covenant that he made with Abraham:
   the oath that he swore to Isaac,

10. And confirmed it to Jacob as a statute:
    to Israel as an everlasting covenant,

11. Saying 'I will give you the land of Canaan:
    to be the portion of your inheritance',

12. And that when they were but few:
    little in number and aliens in the land.

13. They wandered from nation to nation:
    from one people and kingdom to another.

14. He suffered no man to do them wrong:
    but reproved even kings for their sake,

15. Saying 'Touch not my anointed:
    and do my prophets no harm'.

16. Then he called down a famine on the land:
    and destroyed the bread that was their stay.

17. But he had sent a man ahead of them:
    Joseph who was sold into slavery,

18. Whose feet they fastened with fetters:
    and thrust his neck into a hoop of iron.

19. Till the time that his words proved true:
    he was tested by the Lord's command.

20. Then the king sent and loosed him:
    the ruler of nations set him free;

21. He made him master of his household:
    and ruler over all his possessions,

22. To rebuke his officers at will:
    and to teach his counsellors wisdom.

23. Then Israel came into Egypt:
    and Jacob dwelt in the land of Ham.

24. There the Lord made his people fruitful:
    too numerous for their enemies,

25. Whose hearts he turned to hate his people:
    and to deal deceitfully with his servants.

26. Then he sent Moses his servant:
    And Aaron whom he had chosen.

27. Through them he manifested his signs:
    and his wonders in the land of Ham.
28. He sent darkness, and it was dark:
    yet they would not obey his commands.
29. He turned their waters into blood:
    and slew the fish therein.
30. Their country swarmed with frogs:
    even the inner chambers of their kings.
31. He spoke the word, and there came great swarms of flies:
    and gnats within all their borders.
32. He sent them storms of hail:
    and darts of fire into their land.
33. He struck their vines and their fig-trees:
    and shattered the trees within their borders.
34. He commanded, and there came grasshoppers:
    and young locusts without number.
35. They ate up every green thing in the land:
    and devoured the fruit of the soil.
36. He smote all the first-born in their land:
    the first-fruits of all their manhood.
37. He brought Israel out with silver and with gold:
    and not one among their tribes was seen to stumble.
38. Egypt was glad at their going:
    for dread of Israel had fallen upon them.
39. He spread out a cloud for a covering:
    and fire to lighten the night.
40. The people asked, and he brought them quails:
    And satisfied them with the bread from heaven.
41. He opened a rock, so that the waters gushed:
    and ran in the parched land like a river.
42. For he had remembered his holy word:
    that he gave to Abraham his servant.

43. So he led out his people with rejoicing:
      his chosen ones with shouts of joy;
44. He gave them the land of the nations:
      and they took possession of the fruit of other men's toil,
45. So that they might keep his statutes:
      and faithfully obey his laws. O praise the Lord.

Psalm 106

1. Praise the Lord;
      O give thanks to the Lord, for he is good:
   and his mercy endures for ever.
2. Who can express the mighty acts of the Lord:
      or fully voice his praise?
3. Blessed are those who act according to justice:
      who at all times do the right.
4. Remember me, O Lord,
      when you visit your people with your favour:
   and come to me also with your salvation,
5. That I may see the prosperity of your chosen:
      that I may rejoice with the rejoicing of your people,
   and exult with those who are your own.
6. We have sinned like our fathers:
      we have acted perversely and done wrong.
7. Our fathers when they were in Egypt:
      took no heed of your wonders;
8. They did not remember
      the multitude of your loving-kindnesses:
   but they rebelled at the Red Sea.
9. Nevertheless, he saved them for his name's sake:
      that he might make known his power.
10. He commanded the Red Sea, and it dried up:
      and he led them through the deep as through a desert.

11. He delivered them from the hand of their adversary:
    and redeemed them from the power of the enemy.

12. The waters closed over their oppressors:
    so that not one was left alive.

13. Then they believed his words:
    and sang him songs of praise.

14. But in a little while they forgot what he had done:
    and would wait for his counsel no more.

15. Greed took hold of them in the desert:
    and they put God to the test in the wilderness.

16. So he gave them that which they desired:
    but sent a wasting sickness among them.

17. Then they grew envious of Moses in the camp:
    and of Aaron, the holy one of the Lord;

18. Whereupon the earth opened and swallowed up Dathan:
    it closed over the company of Abiram;

19. Fire flared out against their number:
    and flame devoured the ungodly.

20. At Horeb they made themselves a calf:
    and bowed down in worship to an image.

21. And so they exchanged the glory of God:
    for the likeness of an ox that eats hay.

22. They forgot God who was their saviour:
    that had done such great things in Egypt,

23. Who had worked his wonders in the land of Ham:
    and his terrible deeds at the Red Sea.

24. Therefore he thought to destroy them:
    had not Moses his servant stood before him in the breach,
    to turn away his wrath from destroying them.

25. Then they despised the pleasant land:
    and put no faith in his promise,

26. But murmured in their tents:
      and would not obey the voice of the Lord.
27. So he lifted his hand to swear an oath against them:
      that he would strike them down in the wilderness,
28. And cast out their children among the nations:
      and scatter them through all the lands.
29. Then they joined themselves to the Baal of Peor:
      and ate things sacrificed to gods that have no life.
30. They provoked him to anger with their wanton deeds:
      and plague broke out among them.
31. Then stood up Phinehas and interposed:
      and so the plague was ended;
32. And that was counted to him for righteousness:
      throughout all generations for evermore.
33. They angered God also at the waters of Meribah:
      so that Moses suffered for their misdeeds;
34. For they had embittered his spirit:
      and he spoke rashly with his lips.
35. They did not destroy the peoples:
      as the Lord had commanded them to do,
36. But they mingled themselves with the heathen:
      and learned to follow their ways.
37. They worshipped foreign idols:
      and these became their snare,
38. So that they sacrificed their sons:
      and their own daughters to demons.
39. They shed innocent blood:
      even the blood of their own sons and daughters,
40. Whom they offered to the idols of Canaan:
      and the land was defiled with blood.
41. They made themselves foul by their acts:
      and with wanton deeds whored after strange gods.

42. Then was the wrath of the Lord
     kindled against his people:
   and he loathed his own possession;

43. He gave them into the hands of the nations:
     and their adversaries ruled over them.

44. Their enemies became their oppressors:
     and they were brought into subjection
   beneath their power.

45. Many a time he saved them:
     but they rebelled against him to follow their own designs
   and were brought down by their wickedness.

46. Nevertheless, he looked on their distress:
     when he heard their loud crying.

47. He remembered his covenant with them:
     and relented,
   according to the abundance of his loving-kindness.

48. And he caused them to be pitied:
     even by those that held them captive.

49. Save us, O Lord our God,
   and gather us from among the nations:
     that we may give thanks to your holy name,
     and make our boast in your praises.

50. Blessed be the Lord, the God of Israel,
     from everlasting to everlasting:
   and let all the people say, Amen. Praise the Lord.

Psalm 107

1. O give thanks to the Lord, for he is good:
     for his loving mercy is for ever.

2. Let the Lord's redeemed say so:
     whom he has redeemed from the hand of the enemy,

3. And gathered in from every land,
     from the east and from the west:
   from the north and from the south.

4. Some went astray in the wilderness and in the desert:
    and found no path to an inhabited city;
5. They were hungry and thirsty:
    and their heart fainted within them.
6. Then they cried to the Lord in their distress:
    and he took them out of their trouble.
7. He led them by the right path:
    till they came to an inhabited city.
8. *Let them thank the Lord for his goodness:*
    and for the wonders that he does for the children of men;
9. *For he satisfies the thirsty:*
    and fills the hungry with good things.
10. Some sat in darkness and in deadly shadow:
    bound fast in affliction and iron,
11. Because they had rebelled against the words of God:
    and scorned the purposes of the Most High.
12. So he bowed down their hearts with affliction:
    they tripped headlong, with none to help them.
13. Then they cried to the Lord in their distress:
    and he took them out of their trouble.
14. He brought them out from darkness and deadly shadow:
    and broke their chains in two.
15. *Let them thank the Lord for his goodness:*
    and for the wonders that he does for the children of men;
16. *For he shatters the doors of bronze:*
    and cleaves the bars of iron.
17. Fools were far gone in transgression:
    and because of their sins were afflicted.
18. They sickened at any food:
    and had come to the gates of death.
19. Then they cried to the Lord in their distress:
    and he took them out of their trouble.

20. He sent his word and healed them:
    and saved their life from the Pit.

21. *Let them thank the Lord for his goodness:*
    and for the wonders that he does for the children of men;

22. *Let them offer sacrifices of thanksgiving:*
    and tell what he has done with shouts of joy.

23. Those who go down to the sea in ships:
    and follow their trade on great waters,

24. These men have seen the works of God:
    and his wonders in the deep.

25. For he spoke, and raised the storm-wind:
    and it lifted high the waves of the sea.

26. They go up to the sky, and down again to the depths:
    their courage melts away in the face of disaster.

27. They reel and stagger like drunken men:
    and are at their wits' end.

28. Then they cried to the Lord in their distress:
    and he took them out of their trouble.

29. He calmed the storm to a silence:
    and the waves of the sea were stilled.

30. Then they were glad because they were quiet:
    and he brought them to the haven they longed for.

31. *Let them thank the Lord for his goodness:*
    and for the wonders that he does for the children of men;

32. *Let them exalt him in the assembly of the people:*
    and praise him in the council of elders.

33. He turns the rivers into desert:
    and springs of water into thirsty ground.

34. He makes of a fruitful land a salty waste:
    because its inhabitants are evil.

35. He turns the wilderness into a pool of water:
    and parched ground into flowing springs.

36. And there he settles the hungry:
    and they build a city to live in.

37. They sow fields and plant vineyards:
    which give them fruitful harvest.

38. He blesses them, and they multiply greatly:
    he does not let their cattle diminish.

39. But he pours contempt upon princes:
    and makes them stray in the pathless desert;

40. They are weakened and brought low:
    through stress of adversity and sorrow.

41. But he lifts the poor out of misery:
    and increases their families like flocks of sheep.

42. The upright shall see it and rejoice:
    and all wickedness shall shut its mouth.

43. Whoever is wise, let him observe these things:
    and consider the loving-kindness of the Lord.

Psalm 108

1. My heart is fixed, O God, my heart is fixed:
   I will sing and make melody.

2. Awake my soul, awake lute and harp:
   For I will awaken the morning.

3. I will give you thanks, O Lord, among the peoples:
   I will sing your praise among the nations.

4. For the greatness of your mercy reaches to the heavens:
   and your faithfulness to the clouds.

5. Be exalted, O God, above the heavens:
   and let your glory be over all the earth;

6. That those whom you love may be delivered:
   O save us by your right hand, and answer me.

7. God has said in his holy place:
   'I will exult and divide Shechem,
   I will parcel out the valley of Succoth.

8. 'Gilead is mine, and Manasseh is mine:
    Ephraim is my helmet, and Judah my rod of command.

9. 'Moab is my wash-bowl, over Edom will I cast my shoe:
    against Philistia will I shout in triumph.'

10. Who will lead me into the fortified city:
    who will bring me into Edom?

11. Have you not cast us off, O God?:
    You go not out with our armies.

12. Give us your help against the enemy:
    for vain is the help of man.

13. By the power of our God we shall do valiantly:
    for it is he that will tread down our enemies.

Psalm 109

1. O God of my praise, do not be silent:
    for evil and deceitful mouths are opened against me.

2. They speak of me with lying tongues:
    they surround me with words of hatred,
    they fight against me without cause.

3. In return for my friendship they oppose me:
    and that for no fault of mine.

4. They repay me evil for good:
    and hatred for my affection.

5. [Appoint an evil man to stand against him:
    and let an adversary be at his right hand.

6. When he is judged, let him be found guilty:
    let his prayer for help be counted as sin.

7. Let his days be few:
    and let another take what he has hoarded.

8. Let his children be made fatherless:
    and his wife become a widow.

9. Let his children be vagabonds and beggars:
    let them seek alms far from their own homes.

10. Let the usurer exact all that he has:
    and let strangers plunder the fruit of his toil.

11. Let no man be loyal to him:
    and let no one have pity on his fatherless children.

12. Let his line become extinct:
    in one generation let their name be blotted out.

13. Let the sins of his fathers be remembered by the Lord:
    and his mother's iniquity not be wiped away.

14. Let their sins be constantly before the Lord:
    may he root out their memory from the earth.

15. For he was a man that did not remember to show loyalty:
    but he persecuted the humble,
    the poor and the crushed in spirit,
    and sought to put them to death.

16. He loved to curse—let curses fall on him:
    he took no pleasure in blessing,
    so let it be far from him.

17. He clothed himself in cursing like a garment:
    so let it seep like water into his body
    and like oil into his bones.

18. Let it be as the clothes he wraps about him:
    or like the girdle that he wears each day.

19. This is the Lord's recompense to those that oppose him:
    to those that speak evil against me.]

20. Act for me, O Lord my God, for your name's sake:
    and deliver me, as your steadfast love is good.

21. For I am poor and needy:
    and my heart writhes within me.

22. I fade like a lengthening shadow:
    I am shaken off like a locust.

23. My knees are weak from fasting:
    my flesh grows lean and shrunken.

24. I have become the scorn of my enemies:
    and when they see me, they toss their heads in derision.

25. Help me, O Lord my God:
    and save me for your mercy's sake,

26. That men may know it was your hand:
    that you, O Lord, have done it.

27. Though they curse, yet give me your blessing:
    and those that come against me will be put to shame,
    and your servant shall rejoice.

28. Let those that oppose me be covered with disgrace:
    let them wear their shame as a garment.

29. And I will give the Lord great thanks with my mouth:
    and praise him in the midst of a multitude.

30. For the Lord will stand at the right hand of the poor:
    to save him from those that would condemn him.

Psalm 110

1. The Lord said to my lord:
   'Sit at my right hand,
   until I make your enemies your footstool.'

2. The Lord commits to you the sceptre of your power:
   reign from Zion in the midst of your enemies.

3. Noble are you, from the day of your birth
     upon the holy hill:
   radiant are you, even from the womb,
     in the morning dew of your youth.

4. The Lord has sworn and will not turn back:
   'You are a priest for ever after the order of Melchizedek.'

5. The king shall stand at your right hand, O Lord:
   and shatter kings in the day of his wrath.

6. Glorious in majesty, he shall judge among the nations:
   and shatter heads over a wide land.

7. He shall slake his thirst from the brook beside the way:
   therefore shall he lift up his head.

Psalm 111

1. O praise the Lord. I will praise the Lord
      with my whole heart:
   in the company of the upright
      and among the congregation.

2. The works of the Lord are great:
      And studied by all who take delight in them.

3. His deeds are majestic and glorious:
      And his righteousness stands for ever.

4. His marvellous acts have won him a name
      to be remembered:
   the Lord is gracious and merciful.

5. He gives food to those that fear him:
      he remembers his covenant for ever.

6. He showed his people the power of his acts:
      In giving them the heritage of the heathen.

7. The works of his hands are faithful and just:
      and all his commandments are sure;

8. They stand firm for ever and ever:
      they are done in faithfulness and in truth.

9. He sent redemption to his people,
      he ordained his covenant for ever:
   holy is his name and worthy to be feared.

10. The fear of the Lord is the beginning of wisdom,
       and of good understanding are those
    that keep his commandments:
       his praise shall endure for ever.

Psalm 112

1. O praise the Lord. Blessed is the man who fears the Lord:
      and greatly delights in his commandments.

2. His children shall be mighty in the land:
      a race of upright men who will be blessed.

3. Riches and plenty shall be in his house:
   and his righteousness stands for ever.

4. Light arises in darkness for the upright:
   gracious and merciful is the righteous man.

5. It goes well with the man who acts generously and lends:
   who guides his affairs with justice.

6. Surely he shall never be moved:
   the righteous shall be held in everlasting remembrance.

7. He will not fear bad tidings:
   his heart is steadfast, trusting in the Lord.

8. His heart is confident and will not fear:
   he will see the downfall of his enemies.

9. He gives freely to the poor:
   his righteousness stands for ever,
  his head is uplifted in glory.

10. The wicked man shall see it and be angry:
   he shall gnash his teeth and consume away;
   and the hope of the wicked shall fail:

Psalm 113

1. Praise the Lord,
   O sing praises, you that are his servants:
  O praise the name of the Lord.

2. Let the name of the Lord be blessed:
   from this time forward and for ever.

3. From the rising of the sun to its going down:
   let the name of the Lord be praised.

4. The Lord is exalted over all the nations:
   and his glory is above the heavens.

5. Who can be likened to the Lord our God:
   in heaven or upon the earth,

6. Who has his dwelling so high:
   yet condescends to look on things beneath?

7. He raises the lowly from the dust:
    and lifts the poor from out of the dungheap;

8. He gives them a place among the princes:
    even among the princes of his people.

9. He causes the barren woman to keep house:
    and makes her a joyful mother of children.
    Praise the Lord.

Psalm 114

1. When Israel came out of Egypt:
    and the house of Jacob from among a people of an alien tongue,

2. Judah became his sanctuary:
    and Israel his dominion.

3. The sea saw that, and fled:
    Jordan was driven back.

4. The mountains skipped like rams:
    and the little hills like young sheep.

5. What ailed you, O sea, that you fled:
    O Jordan, that you were driven back?

6. You mountains, that you skipped like rams:
    and you little hills like young sheep?

7. Tremble, O earth, at the presence of the Lord:
    at the presence of the God of Jacob,

8. Who turned the rock into a pool of water:
    and the flint-stone into a welling spring.

Psalm 115

1. Not to us, O Lord, not to us
    but to your name give the glory:
    for the sake of your faithfulness and your loving-kindness.

2. Why should the heathen say 'Where is their God?':
    our God is in heaven, he does whatever he wills.

3. As for their idols, they are silver and gold:
    the work of a man's hand.

4. They have mouths, but speak not:
    they have eyes, but they cannot see.

5. They have ears, yet hear nothing:
    they have noses, but cannot smell.

6. Hands they have, but handle nothing,
    feet, but they do not walk:
  they make no sound with their throats.

7. Those who make them shall be like them:
    so shall everyone that trusts in them.

8. O Israel, trust in the Lord:
    he is your help and your shield.

9. O house of Aaron, trust in the Lord:
    he is your help and your shield.

10. You that fear the Lord, trust in the Lord:
     he is your help and your shield.

11. The Lord has remembered us and he will bless us:
     he will bless the house of Israel,
   he will bless the house of Aaron.

12. He will bless all those that fear the Lord:
     both high and low together.

13. May the Lord increase you greatly:
     You and your children after you.

14. The blessing of the Lord be upon you:
     he that made heaven and earth.

15. As for the heavens, they are the Lord's:
     but the earth he has given to the children of men.

16. The dead do not praise the Lord:
     nor do any that go down to silence.

17. But we will bless the Lord:
     both now and for evermore. O praise the Lord.

Psalm 116

1. I love the Lord, because he heard my voice:
    the voice of my supplication;

2. Because he inclined his ear to me:
    in the day that I called to him.

3. The cords of death encompassed me,
    the snares of the grave took hold on me:
   I was in anguish and sorrow.

4. Then I called upon the name of the Lord:
    'O Lord, I beseech you, deliver me!'

5. Gracious and righteous is the Lord:
    full of compassion is our God.

6. The Lord preserves the simple:
    When I was brought low, he saved me.

7. Return, O my soul, to your rest:
    For the Lord has rewarded you.

8. For you, O Lord, have delivered my soul from death:
    my eyes from tears and my feet from falling.

9. I will walk before the Lord:
    in the land of the living.

10. I believed that I would perish, I was brought very low:
    I said in my haste 'All men are liars'.

11. How shall I repay the Lord:
    for all his benefits to me?

12. I will take up the cup of salvation:
    and call upon the name of the Lord.

13. I will pay my vows to the Lord:
    in the presence of all his people.

14. Grievous in the sight of the Lord:
    is the death of his faithful ones.

15. O Lord, I am your servant,
    your servant and the son of your handmaid:
   you have unloosed my bonds.

16. I will offer you a sacrifice of thanksgiving:
    and call upon the name of the Lord.

17. I will pay my vows to the Lord:
    in the presence of all his people,

18. In the courts of the house of the Lord:
    even in your midst, O Jerusalem. Praise the Lord.

Psalm 117

1. O praise the Lord, all you nations:
   O praise him, all you peoples.

2. For great is his loving-kindness toward us:
   and the faithfulness of the Lord endures for ever.
   Praise the Lord.

Psalm 118

1. O give thanks to the Lord, for he is good:
   his mercy endures for ever.

2. Let Israel now proclaim:
   that his mercy endures for ever.

3. Let the house of Aaron proclaim:
   that his mercy endures for ever.

4. Let those who fear the Lord proclaim:
   that his mercy endures for ever.

5. In my danger I called to the Lord:
   he answered and set me free.

6. The Lord is on my side, I shall not fear:
   What can man do to me?

7. The Lord is at my side as my helper:
   I shall see the downfall of my enemies.

8. It is better to take refuge in the Lord:
    than to put your trust in man;

9. It is better to take refuge in the Lord:
    than to put your trust in princes.

10. All the nations surrounded me:
    but in the name of the Lord I drove them back.

11. They surrounded, they surrounded me on every side:
    but in the name of the Lord I drove them back.

12. They swarmed about me like bees,
       they blazed like fire among the thorns:
    in the name of the Lord I drove them back.

13. I was pressed so hard that I almost fell:
    but the Lord was my helper.

14. The Lord is my strength and my song:
    and has become my salvation.

15. The sounds of joy and deliverance:
    are in the tents of the righteous.

16. The right hand of the Lord does mighty things:
    the right hand of the Lord raises up.

17. I shall not die but live:
    and proclaim the works of the Lord.

18. The Lord has disciplined me hard:
    but he has not given me over to death.

19. Open me the gates of righteousness:
    and I will enter and give thanks to the Lord.

20. This is the gate of the Lord:
    the righteous shall enter it.

21. I will praise you, for you answered me:
    and have become my salvation.

22. The stone that the builders rejected:
    has become the head of the corner.

23. This is the Lord's doing:
    and it is marvellous in our eyes.

24. This is the day that the Lord has made:
    let us rejoice and be glad in it.

25. O Lord, save us, we pray:
    O Lord, send us prosperity.

26. Blessed is he who comes, in the name of the Lord:
    from the house of the Lord we bless you.

27. The Lord is God, and he has given us light:
    guide the festal throng up to the horns of the altar.

28. You are my God and I will praise you:
    you are my God, I will exalt you.

29. O give thanks to the Lord, for he is good:
    and his mercy endures for ever.

Psalm 119

1

1. Blessed are those whose way is blameless:
   who walk in the law of the Lord.

2. Blessed are those who keep his commands:
   and seek him with their whole heart;

3. Those who do no wrong:
   but walk in the ways of our God.

4. For you, Lord, have commanded us:
   to persevere in all your precepts.

5. If only my ways were unerring:
   towards the keeping of your statutes!

6. Then I should not be ashamed:
   when I looked on all your commandments.

7. I will praise you with sincerity of heart:
   as I learn your righteous judgements.

8. I will keep your statutes:
   O forsake me not utterly.

2

9. How shall a young man's path be pure:
   unless he keep to your word?

10. I have sought you with my whole heart:
    let me not stray from your commandments.

11. I have treasured your words in my heart:
    that I might not sin against you.

12. Blessed are you, Lord God:
    O teach me your statutes.

13. With my lips I have been telling:
    all the judgements of your mouth.

14. And I find more joy in the way of your commands:
    than in all manner of riches.

15. I will meditate on your precepts:
    and give heed to your ways;

16. For my delight is wholly in your statutes:
    and I will not forget your word.

3

17. O be bountiful to your servant that I may live:
    in obedience to your word.

18. Take away the veil from my eyes:
    that I may see the wonders of your law.

19. I am but a stranger on the earth:
    do not hide your commandments from me.

20. My soul is consumed with longing:
    for your judgements day and night.

21. You have rebuked the proud:
    and cursed are those who stray
    from your commandments;

22. Turn away from me their reproach and scorn:
    for I have kept your commands.

23. Though princes sit and plot together against me:
    your servant shall meditate on your statutes;

24. For your commands are my delight:
    and they are counsellors in my defence.

4

25. I am humbled to the dust:
    O give me life according to your word.

26. If I examine my ways:
    surely you will answer me - O teach me your statutes!

27. Make me to understand the way of your precepts:
    and I shall meditate on your marvellous works.

28. My soul pines away for sorrow:
    O raise me up according to your word.

29. Keep me far from the way of deception:
    and grant me the grace of your law.

30. I have chosen the way of truth:
    and have set your judgements before me.

31. I hold fast to your commands:
    O Lord, let me never be confounded.

32. Let me run the way of your commandments:
    for you will liberate my heart.

5

33. Teach me, O Lord, the way of your statutes:
    and I will honour it to the end.

34. Give me understanding, that I may keep your law:
    that I may keep it with my whole heart.

35. Guide me in the path of your commandments:
    for therein is my delight.

36. Incline my heart to your commands:
    and not to selfish gain.

37. Turn away my eyes from looking on vanities:
    as I walk in your way give me life.

38. Make good your promise to your servant:
    the promise that endures for all who fear you.

39. Turn aside the taunts that I dread:
    for your judgements are very good.

40. Lord, I long for your precepts:
    in your righteousness give me life.

6

41. Let your loving mercy come to me, O Lord:
    and your salvation, according to your word.

42. Then I shall have an answer for those who reproach me:
    for I trust in your word.

43. Do not take the word of truth utterly out of my mouth:
    for in your judgements is my hope.

44. Let me keep your law continually:
    O let me keep it for ever.

45. And so I shall walk at liberty:
    because I have sought your precepts.

46. I shall speak of your commands before kings:
    and shall not be put to shame.

47. My delight shall be in your commandments:
    which I have greatly loved;

48. I shall worship you with outstretched hands:
    and I shall meditate on your statutes.

7

49. Remember your word to your servant:
    on which you have built my hope.

50. This has been my comfort in my affliction:
    for your word has brought me life.

51. Though the proud have laughed me to scorn:
    I have not turned aside from your law;

52. But I called to mind, O Lord, your judgements of old:
    and in them I have found consolation.

53. I am seized with indignation at the wicked:
    for they have forsaken your law.

54. But your statutes have become my songs:
    in the house of my pilgrimage.

55. I think on your name, O Lord, in the night:
    and I observe your law;

56. This has been my reward:
    because I have kept your precepts.

8

57. The Lord is my portion:
    I have promised to keep your words.

58. I have sought your favour with my whole heart:
    O be gracious to me according to your word.

59. I have taken stock of my ways:
    and have turned back my feet to your commands.

60. I made haste and did not delay:
    to keep your commandments.

61. The snares of the wicked encompassed me:
    but I did not forget your law;

62. At midnight I rise to give you thanks:
    for the righteousness of your judgements.

63. I am a friend to all who fear you:
    to those who keep your precepts.

64. The earth, O Lord, is full of your loving mercy:
    O teach me your statutes.

9

65. Lord, you have done good to your servant:
    in accordance with your word.

66. O teach me right judgement and knowledge:
    for I trust in your commandments.

67. Before I was afflicted I went astray:
    but now I keep your word.

68. You are good, and you do good:
    O teach me your statutes.

69. The proud have smeared me with lies:
    but I will keep your precepts with my whole heart.

70. Their hearts are gross like fat:
    but my delight is in your law.

71. It is good for me that I was afflicted:
    so I might learn your statutes.

72. The law of your mouth is dearer to me:
    than a wealth of gold and silver.

10

73. Your hands have made me and fashioned me:
    O give me understanding,
    that I may learn your commandments.

74. Those who fear you shall see me and rejoice:
    for my hope is in your word.

75. I know, Lord, that your judgements are right:
    and that in faithfulness you have afflicted me.

76. Let your merciful kindness be my comfort:
    according to your promise to your servant.

77. O let your mercy come to me that I may live:
    for your law is my delight.

78. Let the proud be shamed
    who steal my rights through their lies:
    but I will meditate on your precepts.

79. Let those who fear you turn to me:
    and they shall know your commands.

80. O let my heart be sound in your statutes:
    that I may never be put to shame.

11

81. My soul languishes for your salvation:
    but my hope is in your word;

82. My eyes fail with watching for your promise:
    saying 'O when will you comfort me?'

83. I am parched as a wineskin in the smoke:
    yet I do not forget your statutes.
84. How many are the days of your servant:
    and when will you judge my persecutors?
85. The proud have dug pitfalls for me:
    in defiance of your law.
86. All your commandments are true:
    but they persecute me with lies - O come to my help.
87. They have almost made an end of me on the earth:
    but I have not forsaken your precepts.
88. In your merciful goodness give me life:
    that I may keep the commands of your mouth.

12

89. Lord, your word is for ever:
    it stands firm in the heavens.
90. Your faithfulness abides from one generation to another:
    firm as the earth which you have made.
91. As for your judgements, they stand fast this day:
    for all things are your servants.
92. If your law had not been my delight:
    I would have perished in my affliction.
93. I will never forget your precepts:
    for by them you have given me life.
94. I am yours, O save me:
    for I have sought your precepts.
95. The wicked have lain in wait for me to destroy me:
    but I think on your commands.
96. I have seen that all perfection comes to an end:
    only your commandment has no bounds.

13

97. Lord, how I love your law:
    it is my meditation all the day long.

98. Your commandments have made me wiser
     than my enemies:
   for they remain with me for ever.

99. I have more understanding than all my teachers:
     for I study your commands.

100. I am wiser than the aged:
      because I have kept your precepts.

101. I have held back my feet from every evil path:
      that I might keep your word;

102. I have not turned aside from your judgements:
      for you yourself are my teacher.

103. How sweet are your words to my tongue:
      sweeter than honey to my mouth.

104. Through your precepts I get understanding:
      therefore I hate all lying ways.

14

105. Your word is a lantern to my feet:
      and a light to my path.

106. I have vowed and sworn an oath:
      to keep your righteous judgements.

107. I have been afflicted beyond measure:
      Lord, give me life according to your word.

108. Accept, O Lord, the freewill offerings of my mouth:
      and teach me your judgements.

109. I take my life in my hands continually:
      yet I do not forget your law.

110. The wicked have laid a snare for me:
      but I have not strayed from your precepts.

111. Your commands are my inheritance for ever:
      they are the joy of my heart.

112. I have set my heart to fulfil your statutes:
      always, even to the end.

15

113. I loathe those who are double-minded:
     but your law do I love.

114. You are my shelter and my shield:
     and in your word is my hope.

115. Away from me, all you that do evil:
     I will keep the commandments of my God.

116. Be my stay, according to your word, that I may live:
     and do not disappoint me in my hope.

117. Hold me up, and I shall be safe:
     and I will ever delight in your statutes.

118. You scorn all those who swerve from your statutes:
     for their calumnies against me are lies;

119. All the ungodly of the earth you count as dross:
     therefore I love your commands.

120. My flesh shrinks for fear of you:
     and I am afraid of your judgements.

16

121. I have done what is just and right:
     O do not give me over to my oppressors.

122. Stand surety for your servant's good:
     let not the proud oppress me.

123. My eyes fail with watching for your salvation:
     for the fulfilment of your righteous word.

124. O deal with your servant
     according to your loving mercy:
     and teach me your statutes.

125. I am your servant, O give me understanding:
     that I may know your commands.

126. It is time for the Lord to act:
     for they violate your law.

127. Therefore I love your commandments:
     more than gold, more than the finest gold;

128. Therefore I straighten my paths by all your precepts:
     and I hate all lying ways.

17

129. Wonderful are your commands:
     and therefore my soul keeps them.

130. The unfolding of your word gives light:
     it gives understanding to the simple.

131. I open my mouth and draw in my breath:
     for I yearn for your commandments.

132. O turn to me and be merciful to me:
     as is your way with those who love your name.

133. Order my steps according to your word:
     that no evil may get mastery over me.

134. Deliver me from man's oppression:
     that I may keep your precepts.

135. Make your face shine upon your servant:
     and teach me your statutes.

136. My eyes gush out with streams of water:
     because they pay no heed to your law.

18

137. Righteous are you, Lord God:
     and just are your judgements;

138. The commands that you have commanded:
     are exceedingly righteous and true.

139. Zeal and indignation have choked my mouth:
     because my enemies have forgotten your words.

140. Your word has been tried in the fire:
     and therefore your servant loves it.

141. I am small and of no account:
     but I have not forgotten your precepts.

142. Your righteousness is an everlasting righteousness:
     and your law is the truth.

143. Trouble and anguish have taken hold on me:
     but your commandments are my delight.

144. The righteousness of your commands is everlasting:
     O give me understanding, and I shall live.

19

145. I call with my whole heart:
     hear me, O Lord, I will keep your statutes.

146. I cry out to you; O save me:
     and I will heed your commands.

147. Before the morning light I rise and I call:
     for in your word is my hope.

148. Before the night watch my eyes wake:
     that I may meditate upon your words.

149. Hear my voice, O Lord, in your loving mercy:
     and according to your judgements, give me life.

150. They draw near to me who maliciously persecute me:
     but they are far from your law.

151. You, Lord, are close at hand:
     and all your commandments are true.

152. I have known long since from your commands:
     that you have founded them for ever.

20

153. Consider my affliction and deliver me:
     for I do not forget your law.

154. Plead my cause and set me free:
     O give me life, according to your word.

155. Salvation is far from the wicked:
     for they do not seek your statutes.

156. Numberless, O Lord, are your tender mercies:
    according to your judgements, give me life.

157. Many there are that persecute me and trouble me:
    but I have not swerved from your commands.

158. I am cut to the heart when I see the faithless:
    for they do not keep your word.

159. Consider, O Lord, how I love your precepts:
    and in your mercy, give me life.

160. The sum of your word is truth:
    and all your righteous judgements stand for ever.

21

161. Princes have persecuted me without a cause:
    but my heart stands in awe of your word.

162. I am as glad of your word:
    as one who finds rich spoil.

163. Lies I hate and abhor:
    but your law do I love.

164. Seven times a day I praise you:
    because of your righteous judgements.

165. Great is the peace of those who love your law:
    and nothing shall make them stumble.

166. Lord, I have waited for your salvation:
    and I have done your commandments.

167. My soul has heeded your commands:
    and I love them beyond measure.

168. I have kept your precepts and commands:
    for all my ways are open before you.

22

169. Let my cry come to you, O Lord:
    O give me understanding, according to your word.

170. Let my supplication come before you:
    and deliver me according to your promise.

171. My lips shall pour forth your praise:
 because you teach me your statutes;

172. My tongue shall sing of your word:
 for all your commandments are righteousness.

173. Let your hand be swift to help me:
 for I have chosen your precepts.

174. Lord, I have longed for your salvation:
 and your law is my delight.

175. O let my soul live, that I may praise you:
 and let your judgements be my help.

176. I have gone astray like a sheep that is lost:
 O seek your servant,
 for I do not forget your commandments.

Psalm 120

1. I call to the Lord in my trouble:
 that he may answer me.

2. O Lord, deliver me from lying lips:
 and from the treacherous tongue.

3. What will he do to you, and what more will he do to you,
 O treacherous tongue?:
 you are sharp as the arrows of a warrior,
 that are tempered in coals of juniper.

4. Alas for me, I am like a stranger in Meshech:
 like one who dwells amidst the tents of Kedar.

5. My soul has been too long:
 among those who are enemies to peace.

6. I am for peace, but when I speak of it:
 they make themselves ready for war.

Psalm 121

1. I lift up my eyes to the hills:
 but where shall I find help?

2. My help comes from the Lord:
    who has made heaven and earth.

3. He will not suffer your foot to stumble:
    and he who watches over you will not sleep.

4. Be sure he who has charge of Israel:
    will neither slumber nor sleep.

5. The Lord himself is your keeper:
    the Lord is your defence upon your right hand;

6. The sun shall not strike you by day:
    nor shall the moon by night.

7. The Lord will defend you from all evil:
    it is he who will guard your life.

8. The Lord will defend your going out and your coming in:
    from this time forward for evermore.

Psalm 122

1. I was glad when they said to me:
    'Let us go to the house of the Lord.'

2. And now our feet are standing:
    within your gates, O Jerusalem;

3. Jerusalem which is built as a city:
    where the pilgrims gather in unity.

4. There the tribes go up, the tribes of the Lord:
    as he commanded Israel,
  to give thanks to the name of the Lord.

5. There are set thrones of judgement:
    the thrones of the house of David.

6. O pray for the peace of Jerusalem:
    may those who love you prosper.

7. Peace be within your walls:
    and prosperity in your palaces.

8. For the sake of my brothers and companions:
    I will pray that peace be with you.

9. For the sake of the house of the Lord our God:
   I will seek for your good.

Psalm 123

1. To you I lift up my eyes:
   you who are enthroned in the heavens.

2. As the eyes of servants look to the hand of their master:
   or as the eyes of a maid toward the hand of her mistress,

3. So our eyes look to the Lord our God:
   until he show us his mercy.

4. Have mercy upon us, O Lord, have mercy upon us:
   for we have had our fill of derision.

5. Our souls overflow with the mockery of those at ease:
   and with the contempt of the proud.

Psalm 124

1. If the Lord had not been on our side, now may Israel say:
   if the Lord had not been on our side,
   when men rose up against us,

2. Then they would have swallowed us alive:
   when their anger was kindled against us.

3. Then the waters would have overwhelmed us,
   and the torrent gone over us:
   the raging waters would have gone clean over us.

4. But praised be the Lord:
   who has not given us as a prey to their teeth.

5. We have escaped like a bird from the snare of the fowler:
   the snare is broken, and we have gone free.

6. Our help is in the name of the Lord:
   who has made heaven and earth.

Psalm 125

1. Those who put their trust in the Lord
    shall be as Mount Zion:
  which cannot be shaken, but endures for ever.

2. As the mountains stand about Jerusalem,
    so stands the Lord about his people:
  from this time forward for evermore.

3. For the sceptre of wickedness shall have no sway
    over the land apportioned to the righteous:
  lest the righteous set their hands to do evil.

4. Do good, O Lord, to those who are good:
    to those that are upright in heart.

5. As for those who turn aside to crooked ways,
    let the Lord lead them away with the evildoers:
  and in Israel let there be peace.

Psalm 126

1. When the Lord turned again the fortunes of Zion:
    then were we like men restored to life.

2. Then was our mouth filled with laughter:
    and our tongue with singing.

3. Then said they among the heathen:
    'The Lord has done great things for them.'

4. Truly the Lord has done great things for us:
    and therefore we rejoiced.

5. Turn again our fortunes, O Lord:
    as the streams return to the dry south.

6. Those that sow in tears:
    shall reap with songs of joy.

7. He who goes out weeping, bearing the seed:
    shall come again in gladness,
  bringing his sheaves with him.

Psalm 127

1. Unless the Lord builds the house:
    their labour is but lost that build it.

2. Unless the Lord keeps the city:
    the watchmen watch in vain.

3. It is in vain that you rise up early and go so late to rest,
    eating the bread of toil:
  for the Lord bestows honour—and on those whom he loves.

4. Behold, children are a heritage from the Lord:
    and the fruit of the womb is his gift.

5. Like arrows in the hand of a warrior:
    are the sons of a man's youth.

6. Happy the man who has his quiver full of them:
    he will not be put to shame
  when he confronts his enemies at the gate.

Psalm 128

1. Blessed is everyone who fears the Lord:
    and walks in the confine of his ways.

2. You will eat the fruit of your labours:
    happy shall you be, and all shall go well with you.

3. Your wife within your house:
    shall be as a fruitful vine;

4. Your children around your table:
    like the fresh shoots of the olive.

5. Behold, thus shall the man be blessed:
    who lives in the fear of the Lord.

6. May the Lord so bless you from Zion:
    that you see Jerusalem in prosperity
  all the days of your life.

7. May you see your children's children:
    and in Israel let there be peace.

Psalm 129

1. Many a time from my youth upward
    have they fought against me:
  now may Israel say,

2. Many a time from my youth upward
    have they fought against me:
  but they have not prevailed.

3. They have scored my back as with a ploughshare:
    they have opened long furrows.

4. But the Lord is righteous:
    and he has cut me free from the thongs of the wicked.

5. They shall be confounded and turned backward:
    all those who hate Zion.

6. They shall be as the grass that grows upon the housetops:
    which withers before it comes to any good,

7. With which no reaper may fill his hand:
    nor the binder of sheaves his bosom.

8. And none who pass by shall say to them
      'The blessing of the Lord be upon you:
  we bless you in the name of the Lord.'

Psalm 130

1. Out of the depths have I called to you, O Lord:
    Lord, hear my voice;

2. O let your ears consider well:
    the voice of my supplication.

3. If you, Lord, should note what we do wrong:
    who then, O Lord, could stand?

4. But there is forgiveness with you:
    so that you shall be feared.

5. I wait for the Lord, my soul waits for him:
    and in his word is my hope.

6. My soul looks for the Lord:
      more than watchmen for the morning,
   more, I say, than watchmen for the morning.

7. O Israel, trust in the Lord,
      for with the Lord there is mercy:
   and with him is ample redemption.

8. He will redeem Israel:
      from the multitude of his sins.

Psalm 131

1. O Lord, my heart is not proud:
      nor are my eyes haughty.

2. I do not busy myself in great matters:
      or in things too wonderful for me.

3. But I have calmed and quieted my soul
      like a weaned child upon its mother's breast:
   like a child on its mother's breast is my soul within me.

4. O Israel, trust in the Lord:
      from this time forward and for ever.

Psalm 132

1. Lord, remember David and all his trouble:
      how he swore an oath to the Lord,
   and vowed to the Mighty One of Jacob;

2. 'I will not enter the shelter of my house:
      nor climb into the comfort of my bed;

3. 'I will not give sleep to my eyes:
      or slumber to my eyelids,

4. 'Till I find out a place for the ark of the Lord:
      a dwelling for the Mighty One of Jacob.'

5. Lo, we heard of it at Ephrathah:
      we found it in the fields of Ja-ar.

6. Let us go to the place of his dwelling:
    let us fall upon our knees before his footstool.

7. Arise, O Lord, into your resting-place:
    you, and the ark of your might.

8. Let your priests be clothed with righteousness:
    and let your faithful ones shout for joy.

9. For the sake of David your servant:
    do not turn away the face of your anointed.

10. The Lord has sworn to David:
    an oath which he will not break;

11. 'One who is the fruit of your body:
    I will set upon your throne.

12. 'If your children will keep my covenant
    and the commands which I teach them:
    their children also shall sit upon your throne for ever.'

13. For the Lord has chosen Zion for himself:
    he has desired it for his habitation.

14. 'This shall be my resting-place for ever:
    here will I dwell, for my delight is in her.

15. 'I will bless her provisions with abundance:
    I will satisfy her poor with bread.

16. 'I will clothe her priests with salvation:
    and her faithful ones shall shout for joy.

17. 'There will I make a horn to sprout
    for the family of David:
    I have prepared a lamp for my anointed.

18. 'As for his enemies, I will cover them with shame:
    but upon his head shall his crown be bright.'

Psalm 133

1. Behold how good and how lovely it is:
    when brothers live together in unity.

2. It is fragrant as oil upon the head,
     that runs down over the beard:
   fragrant as oil upon the beard of Aaron,
     that ran down over the collar of his robe.

3. It is like a dew of Hermon:
     Like the dew that falls upon the hill of Zion.

4. For there the Lord has commanded his blessing:
     which is life for evermore.

Psalm 134

1. Come bless the Lord, all you servants of the Lord:
     you that by night stand in the house of our God.

2. Lift up your hands toward the holy place
     and bless the Lord:
   may the Lord bless you from Zion,
     the Lord who made heaven and earth.

Psalm 135

1. Praise the Lord, praise the name of the Lord:
     praise him, you servants of the Lord,

2. Who stand in the house of the Lord:
     in the courts of the house of our God.

3. Praise the Lord, for the Lord is gracious:
     Sing praises to his name, for it is good.

4. For the Lord has chosen Jacob for himself:
     and Israel as his own possession.

5. I know that the Lord is great:
     and that our Lord is above all gods.

6. He does whatever he wills, in heaven and upon the earth:
     in the seas and in the great depths.

7. He brings up clouds from the ends of the earth:
     he makes lightning for the rain
   and brings the wind out of his storehouses.

8. He struck down the firstborn of Egypt:
 both man and beast alike.

9. He sent signs and wonders into your midst, O Egypt:
 against Pharaoh and against all his servants.

10. He struck down great nations:
 and slew mighty kings,

11. Sihon, king of the Amorites, and Og, the king of Bashan:
 and all the princes of Canaan.

12. He made over their land as a heritage:
 a heritage for Israel his people.

13. O Lord, your name shall endure for ever:
 so shall your renown, throughout all generations.

14. For the Lord will vindicate his people:
 he will take pity on his servants.

15. As for the idols of the nations,
   they are but silver and gold:
 the work of a man's hand.

16. They have mouths, but speak not:
 they have eyes, but they cannot see.

17. They have ears, yet hear nothing:
 there is no breath in their nostrils.

18. Those who make them shall be like them:
 so shall everyone that trusts in them.

19. Bless the Lord, O house of Israel:
 bless the Lord, O house of Aaron.

20. Bless the Lord, O house of Levi:
 you that fear the Lord, bless the Lord.

21. Blessed be the Lord from Zion:
 he that dwells in Jerusalem. Praise the Lord.

Psalm 136

1. O give thanks to the Lord, for he is good:
 for his mercy endures for ever.

2. O give thanks to the God of gods:
    for his mercy endures for ever.

3. O give thanks to the Lord of lords:
    for his mercy endures for ever;

4. To him who alone does great wonders:
    for his mercy endures for ever;

5. Who by wisdom made the heavens:
    for his mercy endures for ever;

6. Who stretched out the earth upon the waters:
    for his mercy endures for ever;

7. Who made the great lights:
    for his mercy endures for ever

8. The sun to rule the day:
    for his mercy endures for ever,

9. The moon and the stars to govern the night:
    for his mercy endures for ever;

10. Who struck down Egypt and its firstborn:
    for his mercy endures for ever;

11. Who brought out Israel from among them:
    For his mercy endures for ever,

12. With a strong hand and with outstretched arm:
    for his mercy endures for ever;

13. Who divided the Red Sea into two parts:
    for his mercy endures for ever,

14. And made Israel pass through the midst of it:
    for his mercy endures for ever;

15. Who cast off Pharaoh and his host into the Red Sea:
    for his mercy endures for ever;

16. Who led his people through the wilderness:
    for his mercy endures for ever;

17. Who struck down great kings:
    for his mercy endures for ever;

18. Who slew mighty kings:
    for his mercy endures for ever,

19. Sihon, king of the Amorites:
    for his mercy endures for ever,

20. And Og, the king of Bashan:
    For his mercy endures for ever;

21. Who made over their land as a heritage:
    For his mercy endures for ever,

22. As a heritage for Israel, his servant:
    for his mercy endures for ever;

23. Who remembered us in our humiliation:
    for his mercy endures for ever,

24. And delivered us from our enemies:
    for his mercy endures for ever;

25. Who gives food to all that lives:
    for his mercy endures for ever.

26. O give thanks to the God of heaven:
    for his mercy endures for ever.

Psalm 137

1. By the waters of Babylon we sat down and wept:
    when we remembered Zion.

2. As for our harps we hung them up:
    upon the trees that are in that land.

3. For there those who led us away captive
        required of us a song:
    and those who had despoiled us demanded mirth,
        saying 'Sing us one of the songs of Zion'.

4. How can we sing the Lord's song in a strange land?

5. If I forget you, O Jerusalem:
    let my right hand forget its mastery.

6. Let my tongue cling to the roof of my mouth:
        if I do not remember you,
    if I do not prefer Jerusalem above my chief joy.

7. [Remember, O Lord, against the Edomites
    the day of Jerusalem:
  how they said 'Down with it, down with it,
    raze it to its foundations.'

8. O daughter of Babylon, you that lay waste:
    happy shall he be who serves you as you have served us;

9. Happy shall he be who takes your little ones:
    and dashes them against the stones.]

Psalm 138

1. I will give you thanks, O Lord, with my whole heart:
    even before the gods will I sing your praises.

2. I will bow down toward your holy temple
    and give thanks to your name:
  because of your faithfulness and your loving-kindness,
    for you have made your name and your word
    supreme over all things.

3. At a time when I called to you, you gave me answer:
    and put new strength within my soul.

4. All the kings of the earth shall praise you, O Lord:
    for they have heard the words of your mouth;

5. And they shall sing of the ways of the Lord:
    that the glory of the Lord is great.

6. For though the Lord is exalted, he looks upon the lowly:
    but he humbles the proud from afar.

7. Though I walk in the midst of danger,
    yet will you preserve my life:
  you will stretch out your hand against the fury of my enemies,
    and your right hand shall save me.

8. The Lord will complete his purpose for me:
    your loving-kindness, O Lord, endures for ever;
  do not forsake the work of your own hands.

Psalm 139

1. O Lord, you have searched me out and known me:
    you know when I sit or when I stand,
   you comprehend my thoughts long before.

2. You discern my path and the places where I rest:
    you are acquainted with all my ways.

3. For there is not a word on my tongue:
    but you, Lord, know it altogether.

4. You have encompassed me behind and before:
    and have laid your hand upon me.

5. Such knowledge is too wonderful for me:
    so high that I cannot endure it.

6. Where shall I go from your spirit:
    or where shall I flee from your presence?

7. If I ascend into heaven you are there:
    if I make my bed in the grave you are there also.

8. If I spread out my wings towards the morning:
    or dwell in the uttermost parts of the sea,

9. Even there your hand shall lead me:
    and your right hand shall hold me.

10. If I say 'Surely the darkness will cover me:
    and the night will enclose me',

11. The darkness is no darkness with you,
     but the night is as clear as the day:
    the darkness and the light are both alike.

12. For you have created my inward parts:
    You knit me together in my mother's womb.

13. I will praise you, for you are to be feared:
    fearful are your acts, and wonderful your works.

14. You knew my soul,
    and my bones were not hidden from you:

       when I was formed in secret,
          and woven in the depths of the earth.

15. Your eyes saw my limbs when they were yet imperfect:
    and in your book were all my members written;

16. Day by day they were fashioned:
    And not one was late in growing.

17. How deep are your thoughts to me, O God:
    and how great is the sum of them!

18. Were I to count them,
    they are more in number than the sand:
    were I to come to the end, I would still be with you.

19. [If only you would slay the wicked, O God:
    if only the men of blood would depart from me!

20. For they affront you by their evil:
    And your enemies exalt themselves against you.

21. Do I not hate them, O Lord, that hate you:
    do I not loathe those who rebel against you?

22. I hate them with a perfect hatred:
    They have become my enemies.]

23. Search me out, O God, and know my heart:
    Put me to the proof and know my thoughts.

24. Look well lest there be any way of wickedness in me:
    and lead me in the way that is everlasting.

Psalm 140

1. Deliver me, O Lord, from evil men:
    and preserve me from violent men.

2. Who devise mischief in their hearts:
    who stir up enmity day by day.

3. They have sharpened their tongues like a serpent's:
    and the venom of asps is under their lips.

The Psalms

4. Keep me, O Lord, from the power of the wicked:
    preserve me from violent men,
   who think to thrust me from my course.

5. The arrogant have laid a snare for me,
    and rogues have stretched the net:
   they have set traps along my way.

6. But I have said to the Lord 'You are my God':
    Hear, O Lord, the voice of my pleading.

7. O Lord my God and my sure stronghold:
    You have covered my head in the day of battle.

8. Do not fulfil, O Lord, the desire of the wicked:
    nor further the evil that he has devised.

9. [Let not those that beset me lift their heads:
    but let the mischief that is on their lips bury them.

10. Let hot burning coals be poured upon them:
     Let them be plunged into that miry pit
    from which they shall never arise.

11. Let no man of evil tongue find footing in the land:
     the evil, the violent man - let him be hunted to the end.]

12. I know that the Lord will work justice for the oppressed:
     and right judgements for the poor.

13. Surely the righteous shall have cause to praise your name:
     and the just shall dwell in your sight.

Psalm 141

1. O Lord, I call to you, make haste to help me:
    and hear my voice when I cry.

2. Let my prayer be as incense before you:
    And the lifting up of my hands as the evening sacrifice.

3. Set a guard, O Lord, on my mouth:
    and keep the door of my lips.

4. Let not my heart incline to evil speech,
　　to join in wickedness with wrongdoers:
　let me not taste the pleasures of their table.

5. But let the righteous man chastise me:
　　and the faithful man rebuke me.

6. Let not the oil of the wicked anoint my head:
　　for I pray to you still against their wickedness.

7. They shall be cast down
　　by that Mighty One who is their judge:
　and how pleasing shall my words be to them then!

8. As when a farmer breaks the ground:
　　so shall their bones lie scattered at the mouth of Sheol.

9. But my eyes look to you, O Lord my God:
　　to you I come for refuge, do not pour out my life.

10. Keep me from the snare that they have laid for me:
　　　and from the traps of the evildoers.

11. Let the wicked fall together into their own nets:
　　　whilst I pass safely by.

Psalm 142

1. I call to the Lord with a loud voice:
　　with loud voice I entreat his favour.

2. I pour out my complaint before him:
　　And tell him all my trouble.

3. When my spirit is faint within me, you know my path:
　　in the way where I walk
　they have hidden a snare for me.

4. I look to my right hand and see:
　　but no man will know me;

5. All escape is gone:
　　and there is no one who cares for me.

6. I call to you, O Lord, I say 'You are my refuge:
　　you are my portion in the land of the living'.

7. Heed my loud crying, for I am brought very low:
     O save me from my persecutors,
   for they are too strong for me.

8. Bring me out of the prison-house:
     that I may praise your name.

9. When you have given me my reward:
     then will the righteous gather about me.

Psalm 143

1. Hear my prayer, O Lord:
     in your faithfulness consider my petition,
   and in your righteousness give me answer.

2. Bring not your servant into judgement:
     for in your sight can no man living be justified.

3. For the enemy has pursued me,
     he has crushed my life to the ground:
   he has made me dwell in darkness,
     like those for ever dead.

4. Therefore my spirit grows faint:
     and my heart is appalled within me.

5. I remember the days of old,
     I think on all that you have done:
   I consider the works of your hands.

6. I stretch out my hands toward you:
     my soul yearns for you like a thirsty land.

7. Be swift to hear me, O Lord, for my spirit fails:
     hide not your face from me,
   lest I be like those who go down to the Pit.

8. O let me hear of your merciful kindness in the morning,
     for my trust is in you:
   show me the way that I should go, for you are my hope.

9. Deliver me from my enemies, O Lord:
     for I run to you for shelter.

10. Teach me to do your will, for you are my God:
    let your kindly spirit lead me in an even path.

11. For your name's sake, O Lord, preserve my life:
    and for the sake of your righteousness,
    bring me out of trouble.

12. [In your merciful goodness slay my enemies,
    and destroy all those that come against me:
    for truly I am your servant.]

Psalm 144

1. Blessed be the Lord my Rock:
    who teaches my hands to war and my fingers to fight;

2. My strength and my stronghold,
    my fortress and my deliverer:
    my shield, to whom I come for refuge,
    who subdues the peoples under me.

3. Lord, what is man, that you should be mindful of him:
    or the son of man, that you should consider him?

4. Man is but a breath of wind:
    his days are like a shadow that passes away.

5. Part the heavens, O Lord, and come down:
    touch the mountains, and they shall smoke.

6. Dart forth your lightnings,
    and scatter them on every side:
    let loose your arrows, with the roar of the thunderbolt.

7. Reach down your hand from on high,
    rescue me, and pluck me out of the great waters:
    out of the hands of the aliens,

8. Whose mouths speak perjury:
    and their right hand is a right hand of falsehood.

9. I will sing you a new song, O God:
    on the ten-stringed lute will I sing your praises.

10. You have given victory to kings:
    and deliverance to David your servant.

11. O save me from the peril of the sword:
    Pluck me out of the hands of the aliens,

12. Whose mouths speak perjury:
    and their right hand is a right hand of falsehood.

13. Our sons in their youth shall be like sturdy plants:
    and our daughters as the carved corners of palaces.

14. Our barns shall be full and give food of every kind:
    the sheep shall lamb in our fields
    in thousands and tens of thousands.

15. Our cattle shall be heavy with calf,
    there shall be no miscarriage or untimely birth:
    and no loud crying in our streets.

16. Happy the people whose lot is such as this:
    happy that people who have the Lord for their God!

Psalm 145

1. I will exalt you, O God my king:
   I will bless your name for ever and ever.

2. Every day will I bless you:
   and praise your name for ever and ever.

3. Great is the Lord, and wonderfully worthy to be praised:
   his greatness is past searching out.

4. One generation shall praise your works to another:
   and declare your mighty acts.

5. As for me, I will be talking
   of the glorious splendour of your majesty:
   I will tell the story of your marvellous works.

6. Men shall recount the power of your terrible deeds:
   and I will proclaim your greatness.

7. Their lips shall flow
    with the remembrance of your abundant goodness:
  they shall shout for joy at your righteousness.

8. The Lord is gracious and compassionate:
    slow to anger and of great goodness.

9. The Lord is loving to every man:
    and his mercy is over all his works.

10. All creation praises you, O Lord:
    And your faithful servants bless your name.

11. They speak of the glory of your kingdom:
    And tell of your great might,

12. That all mankind may know your mighty acts:
    and the glorious splendour of your kingdom.

13. Your kingdom is an everlasting kingdom:
    and your dominion endures through all generations.

14. The Lord upholds all those who stumble:
    and raises up those that are bowed down.

15. The eyes of all look to you in hope:
    And you give them their food in due season;

16. You open wide your hand:
    and fill all things living with your bounteous gift.

17. The Lord is just in all his ways:
    and faithful in all his dealings.

18. The Lord is near to all who call upon him:
    to all who call upon him in truth.

19. He will fulfil the desire of those that fear him:
    he will hear their cry, and save them.

20. The Lord preserves all those that love him:
    But the wicked he will utterly destroy.

21. My mouth shall speak the praises of the Lord:
    and let all flesh bless his holy name,
  for ever and ever.

Psalm 146

1. Praise the Lord, praise the Lord, O my soul:
    while I live I will praise the Lord;

2. While I have any being:
    I will sing praises to my God.

3. Put not your trust in princes:
    nor in the sons of men, who cannot save.

4. For when their breath goes from them,
    they return again to the earth:
   and on that day all their thoughts perish.

5. Blessed is the man whose help is the God of Jacob:
    whose hope is in the Lord his God,

6. The God who made heaven and earth:
    the sea, and all that is in them,

7. Who keeps faith for ever:
    who deals justice to those that are oppressed.

8. The Lord gives food to the hungry:
    and sets the captives free.

9. The Lord gives sight to the blind:
    the Lord lifts up those that are bowed down.

10. The Lord loves the righteous:
     the Lord cares for the stranger in the land.

11. He upholds the widow and the fatherless:
     as for the way of the wicked, he turns it upside down.

12. The Lord shall be king for ever:
     Your God, O Zion,
    shall reign through all generations. Praise the Lord.

Psalm 147

1. O praise the Lord,
    for it is good to sing praises to our God:
   and to praise him is joyful and right.

2. The Lord is rebuilding Jerusalem:
    he is gathering together
  the scattered outcasts of Israel.

3. He heals the broken in spirit:
    and binds up their wounds.

4. He counts the number of the stars:
    and calls them all by name.

5. Great is our Lord, and great is his power:
    there is no measuring his understanding.

6. The Lord restores the humble:
    but he brings down the wicked to the dust.

7. O sing to the Lord a song of thanksgiving:
    Sing praises to our God upon the harp.

8. He covers the heavens with cloud,
    and prepares rain for the earth:
  and makes the grass to sprout upon the mountains.

9. He gives the cattle their food:
    and feeds the young ravens that call to him.

10. He takes no pleasure in the strength of a horse:
    nor does he delight in any man's legs,

11. But the Lord's delight is in those that fear him:
    who wait in hope for his mercy.

12. Praise the Lord, O Jerusalem:
    sing praises to your God, O Zion.

13. For he has strengthened the bars of your gates:
    and blessed your children within you.

14. He makes peace within your borders:
    and satisfies you with the finest wheat.

15. He sends his command to the earth:
    and his word runs very swiftly.

16. He gives snow like wool:
    and scatters the hoar-frost like ashes.

17. He sprinkles his ice like morsels of bread:
    and the waters harden at his frost.

18. He sends out his word and melts them:
    he blows with his wind and the waters flow.

19. He made his word known to Jacob:
    his statutes and judgements to Israel.

20. He has not dealt so with any other nation:
    nor have they knowledge of his laws. Praise the Lord.

Psalm 148

1. Praise the Lord, praise the Lord from heaven:
   O praise him in the heights.

2. Praise him, all his angels:
   O praise him, all his host.

3. Praise him, sun and moon:
   praise him, all you stars of light.

4. Praise him, you highest heaven:
   and you waters that are above the heavens.

5. Let them praise the name of the Lord:
   for he commanded and they were made.

6. He established them for ever and ever:
   he made an ordinance which shall not pass away.

7. O praise the Lord from the earth:
   praise him, you sea-monsters and all deeps;

8. Fire and hail, mist and snow:
   and storm-wind fulfilling his command;

9. Mountains and all hills:
   fruiting trees and all cedars;

10. Beasts of the wild, and all cattle:
    creeping things and winged birds;

11. Kings of the earth, and all peoples:
    princes, and all rulers of the world;

12. Young men and maidens:
    old men and children together.

13. Let them praise the name of the Lord:
    for his name alone is exalted.

14. His glory is above earth and heaven:
    and he has lifted high the horn of his people.

15. Therefore he is the praise of all his servants:
    of the children of Israel, a people that is near him.
    Praise the Lord.

Psalm 149

1. O praise the Lord, and sing to the Lord a new song:
   O praise him in the assembly of the faithful.

2. Let Israel rejoice in him that made him:
   let the children of Zion be joyful in their king.

3. Let them praise him in the dance:
   let them sing his praise with timbrel and with harp.

4. For the Lord takes delight in his people:
   he adorns the meek with his salvation.

5. Let his faithful ones exult in his glory:
   let them sing for joy upon their beds.

6. Let the high praises of God be in their mouths:
   and a two-edged sword in their hands,

7. To execute vengeance on the nations:
   and chastisement upon the peoples,

8. To bind their kings in chains:
   and their nobles with fetters of iron,

9. To visit upon them the judgement that is decreed:
   such honour belongs
   to all his faithful servants. Praise the Lord.

Psalm 150

1. Praise the Lord. O praise God in his sanctuary:
    praise him in the firmament of his power.

2. Praise him for his mighty acts:
    praise him according to his abundant goodness.

3. Praise him in the blast of the ram's horn:
    praise him upon the lute and harp.

4. Praise him with the timbrel and dances:
    praise him upon the strings and pipe.

5. Praise him on the high-sounding cymbals:
    praise him upon the loud cymbals.

6. Let everything that has breath praise the Lord:
    O praise the Lord!

You may also be interested in:
Wings of the Morning
by Frank Topping

In this collection of moving meditations, Frank Topping takes as his inspiration verses from the Psalms, St John's Gospel and St Paul's letter to the Romans. With his characteristic sensitivity and honesty he explores the well-loved passages and brings to them a new freshness. Beautifully illustrated with line drawings by Cetra Long, this book is ideal for private reading or group discussion.

"It seemed as if this had been written specially for me," That was the most frequently repeated phrase when listeners to Radio 2 wrote to the BBC asking for a copy of the script of Frank Topping's morning meditations on *Pause for Thought*. "What made me decide to broadcast them regularly," says Frank, "was the huge response from listeners – literally thousands."

In the Frank Topping series, The Lutterworth Press has published many of his most popular radio meditations. These collections of thoughts and prayers remain a pleasure to use and also a handy reference for those who want to find their favourite meditation.

Before being ordained to the Methodist ministry in 1970, **Frank Topping** worked in the theatre and television, both as a producer and a performer. He then worked for BBC Radio Bristol before moving to BBC London in 1974. He is known not only through his radio broadcasts but also because of his West End partnership with Donald Swan in 'Swann and Topping' and his television series 'Topping on Sunday'.

Published 1990

Paperback ISBN: 978 0 7188 2675 8

You may also be interested in:
A Prayer for All Seasons
The Collects of the Book of Common Prayer

A Prayer for All Seasons contains the collects from the Book of Common Prayer. Starting with the collects for Morning Prayer, followed by those for Evening Prayer, and continuing with those for, Christmas, Easter, and other seasons and feasts, and for Saints' Days, and concludes with those for Holy Communion. While the prayers themselves date back to the times of Popes Leo I, Gelasius, and Gregory the Great, the wording of the collects was largely written by the sixteenth-century liturgical genius and Archbishop Thomas Cranmer, the main author of the Book of Common Prayer.

The wonderful collects in the book are framed by early-twentieth-century wood engravings by Blanche McManus which augment and enhance the beauty of the language. Time and faith have hallowed the Book of Common Prayer as one of the supreme achievements of the English language with its splendour.

In addition to a Foreword by the former Prince of Wales, Prince Charles, the book contains an introduction by Ian Curteis, and an Afterword by The Right Reverend Richard Chartres, former Bishop of London.

'This slim and beautiful book reminds us that the Collects are, in their original form, both holy and beautiful. They have a transcendent spiritual radiance that can hardly fail to appeal.'
- **Choir Schools Today**, No. 16, 2002

Published 2024

Paperback ISBN: 978 0 7188 9756 7
ePUB: 978 0 7188 9755 0
PDF ISBN: 978 0 7188 9754 3

BV - #0070 - 051225 - C0 - 229/152/12 - PB - 9780718897710 - Matt Lamination